Lang Fafa Dampha

I0412527

The United Nations Organisation
and African Reparation.

By the same author

1) Nationalism and Reparation in West Africa, L'Harmattan, April 2013.
2) *Afrique subsaharienne : mémoire, histoire et réparation,* L'Harmattan, June 2013.
3) Reparation for Slavery and Colonialism: the Teachings of Durban, Amazon (Createspace), March 2015.
4) Alien Attitude (novel), Amazon (CreateSpace), July 2015.
5) African Migrants (novel), Amazon (Createspace), August 2015.
6) Sub-Saharan Africa and the Bretton Woods Institutions (CreateSpace), December 2015.

This book is dedicated to my late beloved paternal grandmother and friend,
Mba Fatou (Keba) Jammeh.
Rest in Heaven.

Table of Contents

Introduction

Africa had undergone centuries of slave trading, followed by more than 60 years of colonisation and 46 years of Apartheid, which deprived it of its natural unassailable rights. These institutions of oppression and exploitation practically dismantled Africa's pre-colonial socio-economic structures, therefore the freedom to decide and manage its own affairs, and hence its liberty and independence, because the systems that had been functioning normally experienced essential transformations.

At the dawn of the 1940s, however, colonialism in Africa was heading towards its end, thanks to the struggles led by African nationalists, who considered it as occupation and economic and political exploitation. African nationalists continued to strengthen their position in this period, especially towards the beginning of World War II, because the colonial powers were facing serious impediments. The obligatory participation of African soldiers in World War II to combat Hitler's Nazi Germany and the other Axis countries for the liberation of their colonisers, especially that of France and the United Kingdom, rehabilitated and fortified Africa's struggle against colonialism.

It was, however, only after World War II that a wave of anti-colonial struggles in Sub-Saharan Africa, starting with Osagyefo Kwame Nkrumah's Gold Coast (Ghana), forced the colonialists to hand Africa back its sovereignty. This, as we have just noted, was partly the result of the Nazi invasions, which made the colonialists realise that the African peoples too aspired to a separate and free identity, as had been stipulated in the Atlantic Charter in 1941 signed by the British Prime Minister, Winston Churchill and the United States President, Franklin D. Roosevelt. Article III of the Charter states that the West, particularly the United States of America and the United Kingdom, consider "... the right of all peoples to choose the form of government under which they will live [...] to see sovereign rights and self-determination restored to those who have been forcibly deprived of them." (Reader 676)

The Nazi invasion of Europe that led to World War II fundamentally changed the world. The devastating consequences of the war it generated caused economic and political insecurity in the world, and motivated the Allies[1] to establish the United Nations Organisation (UNO) in San Francisco in 1945.

The Charter of the UNO was written from the goals and principles of the Atlantic Charter, which had adopted eight principles from the Fourteen Points[2] of President Woodrow Wilson. The principles of the Atlantic Charter were intended to guide the joint action of Great Britain and the United States of America (USA) in World War II. Both signatories of the Atlantic Charter put their aspirations on a "better future for the world" on the principles of the condemnation of all territorial annexation, the principle of self-determination of all peoples, international cooperation, free trade, freedom of the seas, arms reduction and the condemnation of the use of force; the text also denounced "Nazi tyranny". The Atlantic Charter thus became the basis of the UNO Declaration, signed on 1 January 1942 by the representatives of twenty-six countries at war with Germany

---

[1] The Allies or Entente Powers were the countries at war with the Central or Axis Powers (Germany, Japan and Italy) during the Second World War (1939–1945).

[2] In his speech to Congress on War Aims and Peace Terms on January 8, 1918, President Woodrow Wilson of the United States of America proposed a 14-point programme as a benchmark for world peace to be used for peace negotiations after World War I. He directly addressed what he perceived as the causes of the World War and called for the abolition of secret treaties, an adjustment in colonial claims in the interests of both native peoples and colonists, a reduction in armaments, and freedom of the seas. He also proposed the removal of economic barriers between nations, the promise of "self-determination" for those oppressed minorities, and a world organisation that would provide a system of collective security for all nations as a way of ensuring world peace in the future. The 14 Points were designed to weaken the Central Powers and inspired the Allies to victory.

and the other Axis countries, and subsequently the UN Charter, signed on 26 June 1945 in San Francisco.

The United Nations Organisation (UNO) or simply the United Nations (UN) was thus founded in 1945, when the bulk of Africa, with the exception of Liberia, Ethiopia and the Union of South Africa, were still under colonial rule. It was, as we have indicated, a response to international problems caused by the two World Wars, particularly the second one, and an attempt to succeed where its predecessor, the League of Nations[3] had failed. The initial goal of the UN was "[...] to save succeeding generations from the scourge of war, which twice in our lifetime has brought untold sorrow to mankind." (UN Charter, Preamble). The Charter also proclaims "to reaffirm faith in fundamental human rights, [...] in the equal rights of men and women and of nations large and small [...] to establish conditions under which justice and respect for the obligations arising from treaties and other sources of international law can be maintained, and to promote social progress and better standards of life in larger freedom." (Ibid) These goals, which incorporated and emphasised the notion of equality and freedom of all individuals and nations, were broad and revolutionary for humankind as a whole.

What is the relationship between Sub-Saharan Africa and the United Nations? What is the role of the United Nations in African reconstruction in terms of socio-economic development?[4]

---

[3] The League of Nations (LN) was the first inter-governmental organisation that existed between 1920 and 1946. It was founded as a result of the Paris Peace Conference that ended World War I. Headquartered in Geneva, Switzerland, its principal mission was to maintain international peace and security. Its primary goals, as stated in its Covenant, were to prevent wars through collective security measures and disarmament, by settling international disputes and conflicts through arbitration and negotiation. The League of Nations achieved some success. Its major failure, however, was that it was not able to prevent World War II; it was the predecessor to the United Nations organisation.

[4] Reconstruction, reparation and development are interchangeably used in this

This work is oriented to the study of Sub-Saharan Africa and its relation with the United Nations; however, references have sometimes been made to the entire African continent, because the nature of African history in this era of post-colonialism is that most regions could hardly be effectively studied without considering the entire continent.

---

work.

The United Nations and African reparation

When the United Nations was conceived in 1945, the African continent had four representatives from a total of 51 Member States.[5] By the early 1960s, with the acceleration of decolonisation in Africa, the representation of Africa within the United Nations increased rapidly. Between 1945 and 1960, Africa's representation jumped from 4 to 24 members, and then to 39 members in 1971. After the accession to membership of Switzerland and East Timor in 2002, the United Nations had 191 Member States. With the membership of South Sudan in 2012, it now has a total of 193 Member States, almost universal. African countries all joined the United Nations immediately after their independence, meaning that the 54 States of Africa are now members of the UN, which corresponds to more than a third of the membership of the Organisation. The spontaneity of their adherence to this inter-governmental organisation, based on the principle of equality of all its Member States without exception, to ensure the security of the international community, is remarkable. But what really is Africa gaining from its membership to the United Nations in terms of its reparation in particular, and its development in general?

The Charter of the UN, a huge document with 19 chapters and 111 articles, broadly defines the structure, role and function of the organisation. Once drafted and signed in San Francisco in June 1945, it established six principal organs. The United Nations "is based on the principle of the sovereign equality of all its Members," the settlement of "international disputes by peaceful means" and refraining "from the threat or use of force against the territorial integrity or political independence of any State." (Article II)

---

[5] Egypt, Ethiopia, Liberia and Union of South Africa were part of the founding members. Poland was not represented at the San Francisco Conference, but later signed the charter and became part of the original 51 Member States.

The intentions set out in the Charter are noble because they are primarily geared to ensuring international peace and security, justice, self-determination and respect for human rights, freedom and the promotion of social progress.

Before analysing the structure and functioning of the UN in its relations with Africa, it is worth studying its immediate contribution to Africa's reparation and development as a first reflection on its role. We have said that the United Nations as a product of World War II was founded to restore stable international relations, and establish peace and international security on a more solid foundation. Peace-keeping therefore becomes one of its main concerns. However, the Charter is more than a simple instrument of peace and conflict resolution. It has created structures and specialised agencies in several different functions and domains of development for the promotion of human rights, education, science, culture, health etc.

To determine the immediate realisations and achievements of the United Nations in Africa since its inception, it is important to examine the problem inherent to the African continent, namely the slave trade, Colonialism and post-colonialism in terms of African reparation. When the UN was founded in 1945, the slave trade was a thing of the past; therefore European colonisation and its attribute, apartheid in Africa, are the starting point of our analysis.

The former Secretary General, Kofi Annan, a citizen of Sub-Saharan Africa (Ghana), in an interview conducted by "*L'Express*" newspaper in partnership with "*Radio France Internationale*" (*RFI*) and "*TV5*", responded to criticisms of which the organisation has been victim, as follows:

> We failed in some cases, but we also realised some success. UN has passed the test of decolonisation. In Namibia, South Africa, Mozambique, it went well. Concerning the humanitarian and economic aspects, the United Nation's contribution has been significant. And in the political domain, we managed to end civil wars, for example the

crisis between East Timor and Indonesia. In Cyprus and Western Sahara, where UN has been present for many years, there has been no more clashes. We were able to convince the international community that there were economic and social reasons for the conflict and that we need to address the root of these problems. It is the same thing for violations of human rights and dignity of the individual, which may, if we are not careful, lead to conflicts. (lexpress.fr)[6]

There is truth in this statement by the Secretary General, especially concerning decolonisation in Africa. The United Nations has contributed enormously to the advent and realisation of decolonisation in Africa. The Trusteeship Council[7], one of its six principal organs, was responsible for administering territories that were not fully independent, put under the care of the United Nations. The creation of this Council right from the formation of the United Nations in 1945 symbolised the desire and determination of some statesmen, whose main voice was that of President Franklin D Roosevelt of the United States of America, to apply the third clause of the Atlantic Charter. Britain would have opposed it, but considering the origin of the United Nations and the paradox that opposing it could generate, the

---

[6] Nous avons échoué dans certains cas, mais nous avons aussi des succès à notre actif. L'ONU a réussi l'épreuve des décolonisations. En Namibie, en Afrique du Sud, au Mozambique, cela s'est bien passé. Sur les plans humanitaire et économique, la contribution des Nations unies a été importante. Et, sur le plan politique, on a pu mettre un terme à des guerres civiles, en réglant par exemple la crise entre le Timor-Oriental et l'Indonésie. A Chypre, au Sahara occidental, où l'ONU est présente depuis des années, il n'y a plus eu d'affrontements. Nous avons pu convaincre la communauté internationale qu'il y avait des raisons économiques et sociales à l'origine des conflits et qu'il fallait s'attaquer à la base de ces problèmes. Même chose pour les violations des droits de l'homme et de la dignité de l'individu, qui peuvent, si l'on n'y prend pas garde, engendrer des conflits.

[7] This Council, whose structure, role and function are listed in Chapter 13 of the Charter of the United Nation, was created to oversee the administration of territories that had not yet fully gained their independence. (UN Charter, Article 86, Chapter XIII.) See also Chapters XI, XII.

principle was incorporated in the Charter. In fact self-determination is actually the second main objective of the United Nations. We will recall that when the founding conference of the United Nations was held, most of Africa was still under colonial rule. The debate about their state and future even divided the Allies, especially the colonialists, Britain and France, on one side and the United States on the other. The United States having been a colony of Britain, which had to fight painfully to obtain its independence, has traditionally been against Colonialism. At least three chapters of the Charter are devoted to the "international trusteeship system, for the administration and supervision of such territories as may be placed thereunder by subsequent individual agreements. These territories are hereinafter referred to as trust territories." (Article 75) The Trusteeship Council was symbolically conceived as one of the principal organs of the United Nations. It suspended its operations in November 1994 when the last remaining trust territory of the United Nations, Palau, obtained its independence on October 1, 1994. The rules of procedure of the Trusteeship Council were subsequently amended by dropping the obligation to meet every year and deciding to meet occasionally as required.

Very recently, in May 2013, the General Assembly of the United Nations reaffirmed its commitment to decolonisation by adopting resolution A/67/L.56/Rev.1 that defended "the inalienable right of the people of French Polynesia to self-determination and independence 'and register' the overseas territories of France on the list of territories to be decolonised, an approach that could eventually pave the way for a referendum."[8](lemonde.fr) This vote took place despite three diplomatic initiatives made by France to try to prevent

---

[8]"le droit inaliénable de la population de la Polynésie française à l'autodétermination et à l'indépendance" et réinscrive "la collectivité d'outre-mer sur la liste des territoires à décoloniser. Une démarche susceptible, à terme, d'ouvrir la voie à l'organisation d'un référendum."

the vote, arguing that the resolution was against "the will of the peoples concerned."[9](ibid)

The creation of the UN plays a role in the progressive independence of the African continent and its insertion in the global community. Beginning as an alliance, the United Nations became an international organisation, welcoming into its ranks newly independent countries, with different cultures and varying levels of development. With the arrival of a large number of newly independent countries, the UN launched a vast and comprehensive programme of poverty alleviation and promotion of development, especially in developing countries in the 1970s. Although, for many years, the North and South had been sometimes involved in contradictory debates in the General Assembly and the Economic and Social Council (ECOSOC) of the UN, these differences began to die away when both parties realised that the process of sustainable development in an international context required cooperation, which is the raison d'être of the UN, rather than confrontation. The UN has largely promoted the process of peaceful decolonisation and continues to play a role in the process of the reparation of the African continent.

The United Nations also greatly contributed to the fight against apartheid in South Africa, a phenomenon that was a direct product of European Colonialism in Africa. The General Assembly imposed political and economic sanctions: embargo on arms and economic and social activities, including sporting events, which contributed to the killing of apartheid. The UN qualified apartheid and slavery as a "crime against humanity," immediately after its inception. Its support of the efforts of the Organisation of African Unity enabled all the peoples of South Africa, without distinction of race, to democratically participate equally in general elections. In collaboration with the African Union, it has

---

[9] ..la volonté des populations concernées.

provided assistance to electoral processes and follow-ups of election procedures in Africa. This effectively allowed several African countries to hold "free and fair" elections and to establish "democratic governments." Namibia, Mozambique and South Sudan, and other African countries received direct assistance from the OAU/AU and the UN, in the process of instituting democracy after their independence.

Over the years, the UN established a set of funds and programmes of development that the founders might probably not have imagined. These programmes are run by the Economic and Social Council, under Article 63 of the Charter, and are administered by the specialised institutions of the UN. The Millennium Declaration of 2000[10] expressed the objectives of building a better world by reducing poverty in the world by half.

It is obvious that no country can engage in an effective process of development in an atmosphere of instability and conflict. Yet Africa is, undoubtedly, one of the continents that have enormously suffered from conflict of all kinds after independence, both in the social and political domains. Nigeria suffered the Biafran (civil) War from July 1967 to January 1970; Burundi and Rwanda endured genocide in 1972 and 1994 respectively; Sierra Leone and Liberia went through more than a decade of civil war between 1991 and 2003, marked by coups d'état and rebellions; Sudan,[11]

---

[10] Between 6 and 8 September 2000, the Heads of State and Government of the Member States of the United Nations gathered at the UN Headquarters in New York for the Millennium Assembly. At the summit, the UN agreed to eight Millennium development objectives, which is a blueprint for building a better world. They are, among others, reducing poverty by half, universal primary education for all, putting an end to the propagation of HIV/AIDS. These objectives are to be achieved by 2015.

[11] The Republic of Sudan split into two countries in 2011 (South and North Sudan) following an independence referendum. The relations between the Northern and Southern parts of Sudan have been complex leading to ethnic conflict, generated by colonial policies that exacerbated the existing ethnic divisions.

Democratic Republic of Congo, and very recently Ivory Coast, Mali, Guinea (Conakry), Guinea Bissau, the Central African Republic and numerous other parts of Sub-Saharan Africa have all been submerged in perpetual bloody conflicts.

The UN has participated a lot in the African continent's resolution of its continuous conflicts and the maintenance of peace and security. Its Security Council has been collaborating with the African Union and mobilising the Member States to participate in deploying forces and observer missions. It has supported local organisations in providing equipment for peace missions, and has helped to restore peace in several countries to allow belligerents to enter into viable and reliable processes of negotiation. On March 24, 2005, the Security Council authorised the deployment of an armed force of 10,000 peacekeepers in Southern Sudan to oversee the peace agreement signed in January between Khartoum and the rebels. In Mali, after the invasion of the northern part of the country in April 2012 by "Islamists" who took advantage of the coup d'état of March 2012 by Captain (later General) Amadou Haya Sanogo against the government of the outgoing president, Amadou Toumani Touré, the UN in collaboration with the African Union, the Economic Community of West African States (ECOWAS) and the Malian authorities restored peace and the territorial integrity of Mali.[12] This enabled the organisation of presidential elections in July and August, 2013, followed by legislative elections in November and December 2013, facilitated by the international community headed by the African Union, ECOWAS and the United Nations.

Thus in April 2013:

The Security Council of the United Nations on Thursday

---

[12] This, however, has been hindered by the defeat of government forces in Kidal and the taking over of the city in May 2014 by the Tuareg rebels.

authorised the creation of a peace-keeping force responsible for stabilising northern Mali after the French intervention against the Islamists who controlled the north of the country. Some 12,600 blue berets will therefore take over from the French troops from 1st July. This integrated UN Mission for Stabilisation in Mali,[13] which will replace the Pan-African force AFISMA[14] will be deployed "for an initial period of 12 months."[15] (france24.com)

Previously, resolution 2085 of 20 December 2012, of the Security Council on Mali, authorised "sending an essentially African force of 3,000 soldiers to Mali. The resolution recommends that the Malian government undertakes a parallel process of political reconciliation and negotiations with groups in the north of the country who renounced terrorism."[16] (La-croix.com)

The positive role of the UN in peace-keeping in Africa has been symbolised by its current peace-keeping missions in Africa:

i.   The United Nations Mission for the Referendum in Western Sahara (MINURSO),

---

[13]*United Nations Multidimensional Integrated. Stabilisation Mission in Mali - Mission intégrée des Nations unies pour la stabilisation au Mali (Minusma)*

[14]*African-led International Support Mission for Mali (AFISMA) - Mission internationale de soutien au Mali sous conduite africaine (MISMA).*

[15]...le Conseil de sécurité a adopté à l'unanimité une résolution autorisant le déploiement d'une force de maintien de la paix de 12 600 Casques bleus au Mali à partir du 1er juillet. [...] Le Conseil de sécurité de l'ONU a autorisé jeudi la création d'une force de maintien de la paix chargée de stabiliser le nord du Mali après l'intervention française contre les islamistes qui contrôlaient le nord du pays. Quelque 12.600 Casques bleus prendront donc le relais des troupes françaises dès le 1er juillet. Cette Mission intégrée des Nations unies pour la stabilisation au Mali (Minusma), qui remplacera la Misma (force panafricaine), sera déployée "pour une période initiale de 12 mois.

[16] « ...l'envoi au Mali d'une force essentiellement africaine d'environ 3 000 membres. La résolution recommande que le gouvernement malien engage parallèlement un processus de réconciliation politique et des négociations avec ceux des groupes du Nord du pays qui se dissocieraient du terrorisme.

ii.   The   United   Nations   Multidimensional   Integrated
        Stabilisation Mission in Mali (MINUSMA),
iii.   The United Nations Organisation Stabilisation Mission in the
        Democratic Republic of the Congo (MONUSCO)-
iv.   The   African   Union/UN   Hybrid   operation   in   Darfur
        (NAMID)
v.   The United Nations Mission in Liberia (UNMIL)
vi.   The United Nations Operation in Ivory Coast (UNOCI)
vii.   The United Nations Mission in the Republic of South Sudan
        (UNMISS)

The UN High Commissioner for Refugees (UNHCR) has rescued millions of people displaced by war or persecution, many of whom are in Africa. It has provided means of survival, shelter, medical care and education services. It has helped in their repatriation when the problems that forced them to flee are resolved. On 9 January 2005, the signing of the peace agreement in Sudan, organised by the UN in collaboration with the African Union, ended more than two decades of civil war, which had displaced millions of people in different parts of Sudan, although that has created another state within Sudan.

Some critics have accused the UN of negligence regarding conflicts in Africa, due basically to rival political interests thwarting the Security Council's ability to resolve conflicts in Africa, for example, the Rwandan genocide.[17]

---

[17] Between April and June 1994, at least 800,000 Tutsis and moderate Hutus were massacred in a fever of hatred. The United Nations was accused of doing nothing to prevent the genocide or even stopping it, because they let the atrocities continue. Some accused the United Nations of total inaction, although it was alerted and fully informed of the genocide during its preparation. On April 15, a week after the genocide began, the Security Council of the United Nations decided to reduce the UN contingent to 500 men. During the 100 bloody days that left at least 800,000 Tutsis and moderate Hutus dead, the Security Council never even tried to stop the genocide. Worse, during the massacres, it refused to authorise the sending of more troops to stop this crime. The former Secretary-General, Kofi Anan, who at the time of the slaughter was responsible for the UN peace-keeping operations, recognised the responsibility of the Organisation in the Rwandan genocide.

However if the process of peace-keeping in Africa is partly discredited by dramatic setbacks in Sudan, Rwanda and disappointing results in Angola in the late 1990s, we have seen that other commitments of the UN through deployments of its blue beret peace-keepers were successful in Liberia, Sierra Leone, Mali, South Sudan and the Democratic Republic of Congo, where the UN peace-keeping mechanisms are still actively present, and enabled the government to obtain a major victory by defeating the M23 rebel group in November 2013. Since its inception, the UN has worked for the peaceful settlement of regional conflicts in Africa. In Western Sahara, for example, as stated by the former Secretary General, Kofi Annan, in his interview with "*L'Express*," the engagements of the UN helped stopped the conflict that lasted for several years. Peace and democracy in Liberia and Sierra Leone were acquired through the joint intervention of the United Nations and the African Union.

The United Nations Development Programme (UNDP), in collaboration with other UN specialised agencies and individual African States, operates all over Africa, focusing on the reduction of poverty, Crisis Prevention and Recovery, Environment and Energy for Sustainable Development, to achieve the Millennium Development Goals (MDGs). The UNDP carries out projects in Sub-Saharan Africa to provide policy and programming and technical assistance to individual countries as well as sub-regional and regional organisation. (africa.undp.org) The United Nations considers Africa as a top priority in terms of aid and assistance for development. This is why in 1986 it convened a special session of the General Assembly to mobilise the international community for the promotion of development in Africa.

Through its specialised agencies, the UN spends millions of dollars annually on education, nutrition and health care in Africa. In November 2005, several UN agencies working with the African Union, Non-Governmental Organisations (NGOs) and local authorities in Sudan and Chad provided humanitarian assistance to the vulnerable, especially women and children in the Darfur region. Through the World Health Organisation (WHO), the UN helps people around the world to attain good health, and to ensure that victims of HIV/AIDS[18] and other diseases receive treatment, and that people are informed about the dangers and measures for their prevention. Thanks to efforts by UNICEF, the UN's specialised agency for the welfare of children, and the World Health Organisation, the authority that directs and coordinates health matters within the United Nations system, millions of children each year are immunised against deadly diseases such as measles, tuberculosis and tetanus.

Through UNESCO and other specialised institutions of the UN, more and more adults in developing countries, particularly Africa, can now read and write, while more children go to school. UNESCO has promoted education, culture, science and technology in all the domains of the African society. Its Regional Bureau for Education in Africa with its offices in Dakar, Senegal, usually called by its French acronym BREDA[19], is the largest UNESCO Office in Africa. It is both the Regional Office for Education in Africa, covering the entire Sub-Saharan Africa, and a Cluster Office for Cape Verde, Gambia, Guinea-Bissau and Senegal. It promotes education, social and human sciences, culture, communication and information as a factor of development in Cape Verde, Gambia, Guinea Bissau and Senegal, and education for the entire Sub-Saharan Africa. Through BREDA, UNESCO is committed to promoting development via the promotion of basic and higher education, the planning and development of the system of

---

[18] Human immunodeficiency virus infection/acquired immunodeficiency syndrome.

[19]Bureau Régional d'Éducation pour l'Afrique - Regional Office of Education for Africa.

education, as well as education for peace and sustainable development in Africa.

BREDA supports the efforts of the African Union in the fields of education and the promotion of African languages as a factor of African integration and development. It was within this perspective that BREDA collaborated with the African Academy of Languages (ACALAN)[20] to successfully harmonise and standardise the writing systems of the Fulfulde, Hausa and Mandenkan Vehicular Cross-border Languages in July 2011, in Bamako, Mali. In partnership with BREDA, ACALAN has also begun the process of training trainers of teachers in L1 methodology. The project focuses on the practicalities of implementing the training of trainers "not only to standardise teaching methods in these languages in all the Members States of the African Union where they are spoken, but also to accelerate the process of acquisition of learning skills in the mother tongue."(acalan.org)

The Economic and Social Council (ECOSOC) of the UN, through its resolution 2002/1, "created a framework for advisory group(s) on African countries emerging from conflict with a view to assessing the humanitarian and economic needs of these countries and elaborating a long-term programme of support that begins with the integration of relief into development." (un.org)

The United Nations has been advocating growth in Africa to principally gear towards the continent's priorities, and bring "structural transformation." Consequently, its Economic and Social Council (ECOSOC), in 1958 established the Economic Commission for Africa (ECA) as one of the United Nations' five regional commissions whose mandate, as the regional arm of Africa, is to promote the socio-economic development of the continent by fostering

---

[20] ACALAN is the specialised language agency of the African Union entrusted with the task of developing and promoting African languages in all the domains of the African society and beyond.

cooperation and integration. The Economic Commission for Africa mainly operates in the domains of social development, regional integration and trade, macroeconomic policy, governance, innovation and technology, natural resources and gender. Apart from these main domains of its activities, the Commission equally offers "technical advisory services to African governments, intergovernmental organisations and institutions" on the continent. It similarly formulates development assistance programmes and executes relevant projects. The Economic Commission for Africa delivers advisory services and capacity development support in the priority domains of designing and articulating development planning, implementing macroeconomic policy, promoting industrialisation and the appropriate management of natural resources for Africa's transformation, as well as supporting mineral resources contract negotiations on the continent.

Since the creation of the UN in 1945, its areas of intervention have therefore been numerous throughout Africa: peace-keeping and security operations, coordination of problems of refugees, promotion of literacy and education in general, and the fight against poverty, HIV/AIDS and other deadly diseases. In a nutshell, the UN is almost ubiquitous in the daily life of the African continent, especially in the domain of socio-economic development, and therefore closely and supportively linked to Africa's reparation and development efforts.

The structure and functioning of the United Nations

We have seen that the United Nations has rendered Africa enormous services in the domains of peace and security, education, culture, science and technology. Its positive role in African reparation is therefore obvious and cannot be considered insignificant. However, to determine the real impact of the activities and services of the UN on Africa's development, we have to study its structure and functioning in terms of its operations and in relation to its goals vis-à-vis its Charter, and contrast them with the elements of African reparation and development. Accordingly, the objectives of the United Nations are:

> ...to maintain international peace and security [...] develop friendly relations among nations based on respect for the principle of equal rights and self-determination of peoples, [...] achieve international co-operation in solving international problems of an economic, social, cultural, or humanitarian character, and in promoting and encouraging respect for human rights and for fundamental freedoms for all without distinction as to race, sex, language, or religion... (article 1)

It is worth noting, however, that the United Nations is not a government in the real sense of the term. As an intergovernmental organisation, it has simply been trying to provide the means to help resolve international conflicts and formulate policies on issues of international development that concern us all. All the Member States, regardless of their sizes, wealth or political or social systems have a voice and one vote. It has six main organs, five of which, the Security Council, the General Assembly, the Economic and Social Council, the Trusteeship Council and the Secretariat, are at the Headquarters in New York; the sixth organ, which is the International Court of Justice is based at The Hague, in the Netherlands.

The Security Council of the United Nations Organisation brings together representatives of its executive power and normally works according to the principles defined in Chapter V of the Charter of the United Nations. It is composed of fifteen members, five permanent and ten non-permanent members; the latter are elected for two years by the General Assembly:

> Each member of the Security Council shall have one vote. Decisions of the Security Council on procedural matters shall be made by an affirmative vote of nine members. Decisions of the Security Council on all other matters shall be made by an affirmative vote of nine members including the concurring votes of the permanent members; provided that, in decisions under Chapter VI, and under paragraph 3 of Article 52, a party to a dispute shall abstain from voting. (Article 27)

For votes on matters of political procedures, the veto right cannot be exercised, as a means of allowing the Security Council to discuss a draft resolution even if it is likely that one of the five permanent members will use its veto. Decisions on procedures are therefore made by a majority of nine votes. The other decisions are made by a majority of nine votes, provided that none of the permanent members uses its veto. This veto is a privilege that the five permanent members of the Security Council accorded themselves at the time of establishing the Organisation, enabling each to be able to prevent the adoption of a resolution by a negative vote. It is therefore a special weapon that each of the five permanent members possess to use during votes on issues other than procedural matters, as we have just noted. For example, the United States of America, France, China, the United Kingdom of Great Britain and Northern Ireland, and Russia, each having the power to vote against a resolution as permanent members, can obstruct any proposed resolution that is not on political procedures even if the other four permanent members and all the non-permanent members vote in favour of the resolution.

The Security Council, being mandated by the Charter of the United Nations to maintain international peace and security, deliberates on conflicts and wars. By its resolutions, it condemns and acts on the violations of human rights which constitute a threat or breach of peace and stability to the world. It is therefore responsible for international peace and security and employs a range of measures, from preventive diplomacy to peace enforcement, in accordance with Chapters VI and VII of the Charter. It can force aggressors to end repression by authorising multinational military intervention, and direct the distribution of humanitarian aid and relief programmes. The Security Council does not have exclusive responsibility for the maintenance of international peace and security, but has the primary responsibility for it.[21]

The principles of the structure and functioning of the UN concerning the African continent are that all the Member States are supposed to be equal, as a way of deterring the injustice of men and States, and securing international peace and security for all without distinction, However, membership of the Security Council of the United Nations, which has unprecedented powers, shows that the American continent has one representative, which is the United States of America, Asia has one representative, namely the People's Republic of China, and Europe has three representatives in the Security Council, namely Russia, (former Union of

---

[21]The provision of the General Assembly's "Uniting for Peace" resolution of November 1950 (resolution 377 (V)), is that the General Assembly may act to consider the matter with a view to making recommendations to Members for collective measures to maintain or restore international peace and security, if the Security Council fails to act, due to the negative vote of a permanent member, in the case where there is an act of aggression threat to the peace or breach of the peace. This resolution was resorted to only once. In 1956 the General Assembly established the first and only UN Emergency Force (UNEF I) in the Middle East. The General Assembly did not, however, resort to the resolution when the USA and UK invaded Iraq.

Soviet Socialist Republic), the United Kingdom and France. The latter was not present at the Dumbarton Oaks Conference in 1944, even though it fully supported the principle of collective security of the United Nations. Hence Africa is the only continent that has no permanent representation with veto power in the Security Council of the United Nations.

Originally, in 1945 the 51 founding members of the United Nations were represented by eleven members of the Security Council (five permanent members and six non-permanent members). When the number of members of the Security Council was increased to fifteen in 1963, the United Nations had a total of 113 Member States. In 1999, the number of Member States increased to 188, following the dismantling of the USSR.[22] Of the now 193 Member States of the UN, all 54 States of Africa are members which corresponds to 28% of its membership. These figures indicate that the African continent represents more than one-third of the membership of the United Nations, and is therefore the largest regional group by number, meaning that there is a huge gap between the number of Member States in the General Assembly and the representation of these States in the Security Council. The fact that African countries form the majority in the General Assembly of the United Nations, but have no permanent seat on the Security Council,[23]

---

[22] The collapse of the USSR in December 1991 into 15 separate countries began in the spring of 1990, with the proclamation of sovereignty by Lithuania, Estonia and Latvia, as a first step towards the status of Independent States, followed by Moldova, Ukraine, Belarus and Russia. The disintegration of the Soviet Union was acclaimed by the West, especially the United States, as a victory and triumph of democracy over dictatorship, and confirmation of the dominance of capitalism over communism. It brought an end to the Cold War and transformed the global political situation, leading to an absolute reformulation of political, economic and military alliances all over the world.

[23] Africa has 3 seats on the Security Council, none of which are permanent seats, presently occupied by Chad, Nigeria and Rwanda - currently serving as President of Council. Africa also has 14 seats on the United Nations Economic and Social Council (ECOSOC) and 13 seats on the United Nations Human Rights Council.

shows that the representation of the United Nations does not reflect the principle of equality stipulated in its Charter.

We have noticed that the United Nations was conceived, negotiated and designed around the end of World War II, the most destructive war in human history, to succeed where its predecessor, the League of Nations, had failed, i.e. to avoid a new (world) war. In the aftermath of World War II, the main concern of the States meeting in San Francisco was to prevent a resurgence of German and Japanese threats. During the formation of the United Nations, Africa was not a free continent, but South Africa, Egypt, Ethiopia and Liberia, as we have noted, were amongst its founding members. France, which was absent at the preparatory conference of Dumbarton Oaks, was nevertheless attributed a permanent seat with veto power in the Security Council because it was part of the camp of the Grand Alliance against the Central or Axis Powers, Germany and Japan, in World War II. The Security Council can therefore be considered as a Council of the guiding powers of the Grand Alliance against the Axis:

> The five permanent members were designated in 1945. This position is self-evident for the three guiding powers of the Grand Alliance against Nazi Germany and Japan, namely the UK, the U.S. and the USSR. China is imposed by the United States President Franklin D. Roosevelt, who wants a sound principle in the Asia-Pacific. Regarding France, neither the United States nor the USSR wish the defeated Germany, to become a permanent member of the Security Council, but Churchill, aware that the old Europe is the big loser of the conflict, wants another State of this old Europe to join, there lies its support for France.[24]

---

[24] Les cinq membres permanents sont désignés en 1945. Cette position va de soi pour les trois puissances directrices de la Grande Alliance contre l'Allemagne hitlérienne et le Japon : Etats-Unis, URSS et Royaume-Uni. La Chine est imposée par les Etats-Unis du président Franklin D. Roosevelt, qui veulent un relais en principe sûr dans l'Asie-Pacifique. En ce qui concerne la France, ni les Etats-Unis, ni l'URSS ne souhaitent la vaincue de 1940 comme membre permanent, mais

Seeking a balance in Europe, England therefore wanted a strong France to counterbalance Germany on the European continent. The absence of Germany on the Security Council of the United Nations came, thus, as a form of punishment for its aggression towards the world especially Europe. But if it is normal that the major countries amongst the Allies sit in the Security Council as permanent members with veto rights, the continued dominance of the United Nations exclusively by these Allies through the Security Council, for the simple reason that they were the major military contributors to the victory and the main architects of the UN, is anti-democratic, especially now that the geopolitical situation of the world has changed remarkably. Since 1963, when the last reform of the Security Council was adopted, the composition of members of the United Nations had changed enormously. Its membership has become almost universal now, but the limited number of permanent seats in the Council has remained unchanged. This is contrary to the principles of equality in its Charter, and impacts the proper functioning of the Organisation, almost counterbalancing the tremendous services it is rendering Africa.

The Charter of the United Nations stipulates that the Security Council may, in case of threat of conflict and insecurity, act on its own initiative or at the request of a Member State. If world peace is threatened, it can engage in negotiations, order a cessation of hostilities and the withdrawal of troops. It can also impose economic sanctions and even military action. (Chapter 7, Articles 39-45). These unprecedented powers, however, remain in the hands of only five Member States, primarily European, out of the now 193 Member States of the United Nations, each of which has a veto power to be able to block resolutions. Yet

---

Churchill, conscient que la vieille Europe est la grande perdante du conflit, veut avoir avec lui un autre Etat de cette vieille Europe, d'où son soutien à la France.

the members of the Security Council in most cases, for reasons of political or economic strategy tend to support a United Nations resolution, especially on Africa, generally only if it is favourable directly or indirectly to them:

> Notwithstanding its commitment at the level of rhetoric to the normative goal of protection of civilians, the Security Council's decision-making on conflicts in Africa remains driven mainly by the parochial interests of its five veto-wielding permanent members and their often dissimilar views on sovereignty and non-intervention. (Centre for Conflict Resolution 9)

The five "veto-wielding" permanent members of the Security Council, therefore, generally favour military action only when their national interests or those of their allies are directly at stake. In cases where these national interests are not threatened, and according to their varying views on sovereignty and non-intervention, their actions have often been limited to economic sanctions whose effectiveness is mostly very poor, even if the human cost of the conflict in question is without remission. A classic example is the case of the Rwandan genocide in 1994. The Security Council was accused of remaining inactive until the genocide was nearly finished before allowing intervention. Yet the provision of Chapter VIII of the UN Charter on the rules of cooperation between the Security Council and regional organisations in Africa concerning the maintenance of international peace and security, requires the authorisation of the Council for Africa's own regional peace-keeping activities. The composition and functioning of the Security Council therefore affects, first of all, the strategic interests of Africa in its reparation efforts, and then the notion of equality and democracy, as well as the effectiveness of the United Nations in establishing sustainable peace and security in the world, hence its efficacy, which was more pronounced during the Cold War.

The General Assembly of the United Nations "is the main deliberative, policy-making and representative organ of the Organisation; it comprises all the 193 Member States of the Organisation and provides a unique forum for multilateral discussion of international issues including peace and security." (un.org). Each member has a maximum of five representatives. (Chapter IV, article 9). Each also has one vote "to ensure the equality of all Member States." It is the Assembly General that appoints the members of the Economic and Social Council, the Trusteeship Council and the International Court of Justice. (Chapter 4, Section 10-17) However this Assembly, in which all Member States of the United Nations sit, in view of the equality of all, has almost a consultative role, in terms of international security and peace-keeping. Any country, member or not, can request the services of the General Assembly, but its conclusions are simple recommendations, because the final decision remains in the hands of the Security Council, especially the five permanent members.

The Secretary General of the United Nations is the chief administrative officer of the organisation and its emblem in the eyes of the international community. According to the UN Charter, the Secretary General may be called upon by the General Assembly or any other organ of the United Nations to carry out several functions. The Secretary General may also react independently on matters he or she considers important to maintain the proper functioning of the Organisation. However, the appointment of the Secretary General by the General Assembly for a renewable term of five years is made on the recommendation of the Security Council. By the appointment of the Secretary General, the influence of the permanent members of the Security Council on the United Nations is obvious, even if the fact that the Secretary General never being a citizen of the five members of the Security Council might be considered as a compensation for Member States who do not hold permanent seats in the Council.

The Economic and Social Council (ECOSOC) is responsible for public health, economic, social and cultural education and sustainable development. It also maintains close links with non-governmental organisations in the areas of its jurisdiction under the auspices of the General Assembly. The 54 members of the Council "are elected by the General Assembly for overlapping three-year terms." (un.org) Seats on the Council are allocated on the basis of geographical representation, with 14 seats to Africa, 11 to Asia, 6 to Eastern Europe, 10 to Latin America and the Caribbean, and 13 to Western Europe and others. But, like the members of the General Assembly, those of ECOSOC have an almost consultative role, even sometimes on economic and social issues.

The International Court of Justice (ICJ), consisting of 15 judges elected for a period of 9 years, with a double vote on the General Assembly and the Security Council, is based at the Peace Palace in The Hague, Netherlands. It is the legal weapon of the United Nations, established by Article 92 of the UN Charter and operates on a model inspired by the Permanent Court of International Justice. It is designed as a peaceful means of settlement of any dispute which may threaten international peace and security. It should normally have autonomy in its legal order, since it is the principal judicial organ of the United Nations. To ensure continuity of jurisprudence, judges are renewed by a third, and to be elected a candidate must obtain an absolute majority in the General Assembly and the Security Council. For the principle of independence, there is a geographical distribution of the judges as follows: 3 for Africa, 2 for Latin America, 5 for Western Europe and North America, 2 for Eastern Europe and 3 for Asia. The principle of independence based on an almost even distribution of judges amongst the various regions of the world manifests the will for democracy and equality. Also the adherence of all the Member States of the United Nations to the Statute of the International Court of Justice seems to give it a universal jurisdiction over major conflicts between Member States; however it does not have much authority, as its field of activity has been limited to marginal conflicts. Many States in the 1970s even refused to appear before the Court. Others withdrew from its jurisdiction after judgements unfavourable to them. For example, France withdrew in 1974, when "Australia and New Zealand complained of French atmospheric nuclear testing in the Pacific and considered that these tests were contrary to international law and believed the tests engaged the responsibility of France in their regard since the tests were causing damage."[25] (lawyer-in-herbe.com). The United States also withdrew from the jurisdiction of the International Court of Justice in 1986 after having been condemned by the Court of having "acted in breach of the principle of prohibition of the use of force"[26] in their support to the "Contra," movement, a coalition against the "Sandinistas" pro Cuba/USSR in Nicaragua. (size-prod.com)

---

[25] L'Australie et la Nouvelle-Zélande se plaignaient des essais nucléaires atmosphériques français dans le pacifique et estimaient que ces essais étaient contraires au droit international et estimaient qu'ils engageaient ainsi la responsabilité de la France à leur égard dans la mesure où ces essais causaient des dommages.

[26] …agi en manquement au principe d'interdiction de l'emploi de la force.

The Security Council and the veto power

We have now seen that amongst the six organs of the United Nations, the Security Council has almost absolute power. In fact the powers of the United Nations, especially those concerned with decision making on the maintenance of international peace and security, are concentrated in the hands of the Security Council, without any proper control mechanism of checks and balances; although as we have seen, the General Assembly may act according to the provisions of resolution 377 (V) "if the Security Council fails to act, due to the negative vote of a permanent member, in the case where there is an act of aggression threat to the peace or breach of the peace." Notwithstanding this resolution, the five veto-wielding permanent members can obstruct any resolution, even if it is justified from a humanitarian point of view, and therefore almost control the entire United Nations.

As indicated, it is obvious by the usage of their veto rights, the permanent members of the Security Council strategically protect their national interests and those of their allies more than the overall interest of promoting peace, international security and development. Thus the advent of the Cold War after the signing of the Charter made the functioning of the United Nations problematic. The Cold War divided the members into two opposing camps; and the veto became a way to advance the strategic interests of members of the Security Council or to block those of other members of the UN, and hence sometimes prevents necessary effective action at times of major crises. The Soviet Union and the United States exercised their veto rights as ideological and strategic weapons during the Cold War to deter each other's policies, programmes and system and those of their respective allies; the USSR was more aggressive. Between 1957 and 1985, the Minister of Foreign Affairs of the USSR, Andrei Gromyko was nicknamed Mr

Nyet (Mr No).[27] The behaviour of the USSR and the USA virtually paralysed the functioning and operations of the Security Council for political and ideological reasons.

We have noted that all the continents, except Africa, have permanent representation on the Security Council with veto power. African Member States have only been elected as non-permanent members. The non-permanent membership status of African Member States in the Security Council is a mere formality of presence, because they have no veto power, and specific meetings of the Security Council categorised as "informal" are held without them. Kofi Annan, Secretary General of the United Nations (1997 – 2006), pointed out the undemocratic nature of the Security Council:

> Another major reform envisaged, is the one relative to the enlargement of the Security Council to reflect the new balance of power in the contemporary world [..] The Council, as it is today, is neither democratic nor representative. We have to rectify the democratic deficit, but also review the working methods. A Council which counts 24 or 25 members could not work like a 15-member council. Most Member States are convinced, like

---

[27]Since the ratification of the Charter of the United Nations, the veto power has been exercised 263 times. The Soviet Union (now Russia) used its veto power 127 times. The vast majority of the vetoes of USSR (Russia) have been made before 1991, i.e. before the end of the Cold War corresponding to the Soviet years; altogether 119 times between 1946 and 1991. The United States used its veto 79 times, with more than 40 vetoes related to problems in the Middle East; the majority of the United States vetoes were used to protect Israel. As for the United Kingdom, it exercised its veto power 31 times, the first of which was in 1956 when it joined France in opposing a resolution ordering Israel to withdraw from Egypt. London often used its veto in conjunction with other countries, usually with the United States and France. France used its veto right 17 times, and just as the United Kingdom, its first veto was in 1956 during the war between Israel and Egypt. The People's Republic of China exercised its veto power on 9 occasions only. China's first veto was used in 1955 to block the entry of Mongolia to the United Nations, on the basis that Mongolia was part of China. Each of the four vetoes of Beijing since 2005, were done in unison with Russia. (aljazeera.com)

me, that the UN needs to be reformed, but how? Some insist on the need for a permanent seat for newcomers, while others certainly do not want that. I hope we get the answers by the end of the year, but the negotiations do not look very easy![28] (l'express.fr)

It is important to examine whether an organisation such as the United Nations, which was created to ensure international peace and security and to promote socio-economic development in the world where all the Member States are supposed to be equal, must continue to function with all the continents occupying permanent seats with veto power in the Security Council, except only one deprived of this privilege, which is Africa. What is the impact of this state on African reparation?

Since the inception of the United Nations, amendments to four Articles (23, 27, 61 and 109) of the Charter were adopted by the General Assembly, one of them (Article 61) twice. Amendments on articles 23, 27 and 61 were adopted on 17 December 1963, which came into force on 31 August 1965. Another amendment to Article 61 was adopted on 20 December 1971, and came into force on 24 September 1973. An amendment to Article 109, adopted by the General Assembly on 20 December 1965, came into force on 12 June 1968. The amendment to Article 23 enlarged the Security Council from 11 to 15 members. The amendment to Article 27 provided that decisions of the Security Council on

---

[28] Autre grande réforme envisagée, celle qui est relative à l'élargissement du Conseil de sécurité, afin de tenir compte des nouveaux rapports de forces du monde contemporain... Le Conseil, tel qu'il existe aujourd'hui, n'est ni démocratique ni représentatif. Il faut corriger ce déficit démocratique, mais aussi revoir les méthodes de travail. Un Conseil qui compterait 24 ou 25 membres ne pourrait pas fonctionner comme le fait un Conseil de 15 membres. La plupart des États membres sont convaincus, comme moi, qu'il faut réformer, mais comment ? Certains insistent sur la nécessité d'avoir un siège permanent pour les nouveaux venus, alors que d'autres ne veulent surtout pas de cela. J'espère qu'on obtiendra des réponses d'ici à la fin de l'année, mais la négociation ne s'annonce pas très facile !

procedural matters shall be made by an affirmative vote of 9 members, formerly 7, and on all other matters by an affirmative vote of 9 members, also formerly 7, including the concurring votes of the five permanent members of the Security Council. The amendment to Article 61, entering into force on 31 August 1965, enlarged the Economic and Social Council from 18 to 27 members. The subsequent amendment to that Article, which entered into force on 24 September 1973, increased the membership of the Council from 27 to 54. The amendment to Article 109, relating to the first paragraph of the Article, provided that a General Conference of Member States for the purpose of reviewing the Charter may be held at a date and place to be adopted by a two-third vote of the members of the General Assembly and by a vote of any 9 (formerly 7) members of the Security Council. (un.org)

The modification of the composition of these organs by increasing their sizes logically took into account the increases in the UN membership that has almost quadrupled since 1945, and the consequent impact on its functioning. Therefore we can assume that these increases would ensure a better functioning of the United Nations, in the event that the new compositions, especially that of the Security Council resulted in democratically involving the new Member States in decisions-making, especially concerning peace-keeping and international security. These two assumptions were part of the opinions of Kofi Annan.

The problems of the United Nations with regard to Africa, however, are not due exclusively to the composition of the Security Council. The functioning of the Council, specifically the relative lack of transparency in its work, is also a problem. We have seen that the five permanent members often hold consultations called "informal meetings," which usually precede the general meetings. Most important decisions are actually made during these consultations before the meetings with non-permanent members. Discussions with non-permanent members can therefore be regarded as mere formalities and report sessions of agreements already made during the informal meetings. This situation reasonably creates a sense of marginalisation, and even frustration of non-permanent members of the Council, because it deprives them specifically from participating in a more engaged and democratic manner in resolving world crises.

Article 24 of the Charter of the United Nations stipulates that:

> In order to ensure prompt and effective action by the United Nations, its Members confer on the Security Council primary responsibility for the maintenance of international peace and security, and agree that in carrying out its duties under this responsibility the Security Council acts on their behalf. In discharging these duties the Security Council shall act in accordance with the Purposes and Principles of the United Nations. The specific powers granted to the Security Council for the discharge of these duties are laid down in Chapters VI, VII, VIII, and XII. The Security Council shall submit annual and, when necessary, special reports to the General Assembly for its consideration.

The Member States of the United Nations should therefore be informed of the work of the Security Council, hence the necessity for the Council to function with greater transparency. However it is the confidentiality and lack of openness within the Security Council that undermines its credibility, apart from its lack of democratic representation. To exercise the responsibility of maintaining international peace and security that the General Assembly confers on it, it is essential that the Security Council act equitably on behalf of all the Member States. The informal consultations involving only the permanent members prior to the formal meetings of the Security Council are therefore not a necessity; discussions should be held with the non-permanent members, even if they still do not have the right to veto. As it might be difficult to persuade the permanent members of the Security Council to end their informal consultations, Africa proposed that the reports of the informal consultations are immediately shared with non-permanent members. Some improvements have been made in that the Security Council now holds regular consultations with regional groups and institutions. In this sense, the African Union has established a mechanism for cooperation with the United Nations, intended to better identify the needs of the African continent, especially in the domains of peace and security, to provide effective and swift responses to Africa's problems. Reform of the Council's working methods has also been a major part of the long-running discussions in the General Assembly on Security Council reform. In response to the request of Member States seeking greater transparency in the work of the Security Council, the permanent members of the Council have agreed that the President of the Council inform the non-members of the content and outcome of the consultations as soon as possible. In February 1994, the Security Council accepted that Member States consult draft resolutions after the first month of the same year. The World Summit[29] advocated reform of the Security Council's working methods, recommending that the Council "continue to adapt its working methods so as to increase the involvement of States not members of the Council in its work, as appropriate,

---

[29] The World Summit 2005, which was a follow-up summit to the UN 2000 Millennium Development Summit that led to the Declaration of the Millennium Development Goals (MDGs), was held from 14 to16 September 2005, in New York City. It was considered as the "largest gathering of world leaders in history." All 191 of the then Member States addressed the meeting in some form. If the Head of State or government was not present a representative (Vice President, Deputy Prime Minister, Minster of Foreign Affairs) would speak. The meetings of the summit were presided over by Göran Persson, Prime Minister of Sweden.

enhance its accountability to the membership and increase the transparency of its work." (securitycouncilreport.org) A group of five Member States known as the "Small Five" (S5), namely Costa Rica, Jordan, Liechtenstein, Singapore and Switzerland circulated a draft resolution in 2006 calling for measures to allow better interaction between the Council and the Member States. Although the draft was not put to a vote, consultations on this initiative have continued.

These initiatives and reforms are improvements, but they are not probative democratisation of the United Nations. For the United Nations' decisions to be democratically effective and accepted by the international community in a credible and legitimate way, there should be greater transparency in the work of its Security Council, and the participation of all the continents in the decision making of the Organisation, especially within the Security Council.

The African continent formally constituted the Africa Group at the United Nations, as soon as the Organisation of African Unity was created in 1963, to seek increased representation in the United Nations and other international organisations, consolidate African cooperation and better coordinate strategies on matters of common interest. Previously, Africa represented by Egypt, Ethiopia, Liberia and South Africa as the only independent African States at the time when the UN was being established, was affiliated to the Afro-Asian Group. The increased number of African Member States in the United Nations due to the decolonisation of the continent in the 1960s, has therefore incited the OAU through the Africa Group to reiterate its demand for greater representation and responsibilities within the Organisation. During the Summit of Heads of State and Government of the Member States of the OAU in Harare in June 1997, the Organisation officially confirmed its position by adopting a resolution on the subject in the Harare Declaration. It demanded "at least two permanent seats," with the same veto rights as the current members. This should accordingly also be a way to ensure a better representation in the United Nations. (OAU AHG/decl3 (XXXIII) The African Union (AU) that succeeded the OAU, held two meetings in July 2005, in Sirte and Tripoli, Libya, to determine a collective position of Africa regarding its request for Security Council permanent seats, foreseeing a rotation system based on criteria it had set. The Heads of State and Government of the African Union had handed the matter to a ministerial committee called "the Fifteen" at the Abuja meeting, in January 2005, to examine the whole reform elaborated in December 2004 by a group of personalities of the High Level Panel[30] appointed by the Secretary General of the United Nations. This group had considered two models for the distribution of seats in four major regions of the world, namely Africa, Asia and Pacific, Europe and the Americas:

> Model A provides for six new permanent seats, with no veto being created, and three new two-year term non-permanent seats, divided among the major regional areas. Model B provides for no new permanent seats, but creates a new category of eight four-year renewable-term seats and one new two-year non-permanent (and non-renewable) seat, divided among the major regional areas. (A/59/565)

This first option suggests the allocation of two permanent seats with no veto power, and one additional non-permanent seat to Africa; while the second alternative option based on rotation, allocates two renewable non-permanent seats of

---

[30]Anand Panyarachun, former Prime Minister of Thailand, to chair a High Level Panel of 16 members to investigate the threats to global security and the reform of the international system, 3 November 2003. Among this high-level panel, there were three from Africa, namely Salim Ahmed Salim (United Republic of Tanzania), former Secretary-General of the Organisation of African Unity; Amre Moussa (Egypt), Secretary-General of the League of Arab States and Mary Chinery-Hesse (Ghana), Vice-Chairman, National Development Planning Commission of Ghana and former Deputy Director-General, International Labour Organisation.

four years and one non-permanent seat to Africa. According to this latter, the continent would benefit from the attribution of six seats, two seats for a period of four years and four for two years, non-renewable. This second option thus required the creation of a new category of seats for a four-year renewable term, but they would not be permanent seats. The issue governing the distribution of African seats on the Security Council is considered an African matter which accordingly should be administered by the African Union. In spite of Morocco not being a member of the African Union, the Union should be responsible for the selection of African representatives to the Security Council for permanent membership with veto power

The African Union, however, accepted none of the options of the High Level Panel of the Secretary General. Its Committee of Fifteen renewed its position by demanding at least "two permanent seats with all the privileges and prerogatives for permanent members including the right to veto, and five non-permanent seats." (Ext./EX.CL./2 (VII) This document, called the Ezulwini Consensus[31], was not interested in more non-permanent seats for Africa, but the allocation of at least two permanent seats with veto rights just like the permanent members. The Executive Council of the African Union in March 2005 established a regulatory body, called "the Committee of Thirteen,"[32] which was entrusted to campaign for the promotion of the Ezulwini Consensus, and to negotiate some aspects of the reform. The Committee presented the Ezulwini Consensus to the Secretary General of the United Nations on 25 March 2005.

---

[31]The Elzuwini consensus was named after the valley in central Swaziland where it was made in 2005. The consensus was subsequently adopted at the Extraordinary Session of the Executive Council of the African Union, in March 2005, in Addis Ababa.

[32]Benin, Senegal, Republic of Congo, Chad, Djibouti, Ethiopia, Botswana, South Africa, Algeria, Libya - and Chair of the Executive Council, (Nigeria), Chairperson of the Commission (President Alpha Oumar Konare) and Chairperson of the Elzuwini Consensus (Ghana).

The Secretary General, Kofi Annan being a citizen of Sub-Saharan Africa (Ghana) was considered by many Africans as an opportunity for Africa to gain further consideration in the United Nations; however, this did not have much practical advantage for the continent, due largely to the nature and the functioning of the UN. Since the formation of the UN, the Secretaries General have always followed a cautious path to ensure that they do not upset the most powerful nations.

During the debate of the 47th and 48th plenary sessions of the General Assembly of the United Nations on the reform held on 10 November 2005, the representative of Nigeria, speaking on behalf of the African Group, reiterated Africa's position by expressing the view that Africa could not support or associate with any initiative that would seek a partial reform of the Council. The continent demands at least two permanent seats with all the prerogatives and privileges associated therewith. (AG/10418)

The Africa Group usually speaks with one voice at the General Assembly of the United Nations, but there are no binding regulations to not differ from group positions. The problem is that the Africa Group is treated more like a voting apparatus, therefore slightly feared but not really respected. Even the solidarity or willingness of members of the group, which is the symbol of its strength, is sometimes affected by the lack of a principle to guarantee continuity. The position of Morocco[33] has also affected the group; not being part of the African Union, Morocco has sometimes operated to advance its own agenda at the expense of the African Union, especially during the period Morocco was appointed as one of Africa's three non-permanent members of the Security Council in 2012, in spite of the African Union's nomination of the Islamic Republic of Mauritania for one of Africa's permanent members.

Africa has rightfully linked the number of African

---

[33] Morocco left the OAU in 1984 in protest of the organisation's recognition of the Saharan Arab Democratic Republic's claim to Western Sahara.

Member States at the UN and the absence of the continent as a permanent member of the Security Council with veto power. This perspective on representation is therefore quantitatively based on proportionality, assuming that the representation of the continent in the Security Council must be proportional or at least take into account the number of African States at the General Assembly of the United Nations. This implies that Africa likened the Security Council's legitimacy and democracy to its representation, and that this notion of legitimacy was to ensure greater efficiency. In demanding at least two permanent seats in the Security Council with veto power, Africa naturally seeks legitimacy and equity or democracy, but also to attribute itself influence and control to deter its continuous domination and marginalisation, which has been hampering its process of reparation and development, to which the UN has contributed immensely. This problem is more important for Africa today, because the situation at the Security Council until the end of the 1980s, when the two "superpowers," namely the United States and the Soviet Union, had antagonistic ideologies, could be considered relatively more tolerable for the continent compared with that of today. These two powers assured the balance of power even if they virtually paralysed the functioning of the Security Council with their ideological battles in terms of their political and economic philosophies. Africa did not have to fear too much for being excessively dominated, because each of these powers sought to have its support in some decision-making in international organisations and for some programmes, even if that assurance is only in the short-term and that the situation reduced the continent to a simple voting instrument in the international decision-making process. However, the disintegration of the Soviet Union which brought an end to the Cold War transformed the entire world, leading to a complete reforming of economic, political and military alliances, and leaving no power like the USSR to counterbalance the sole "superpower," the United States. Now the United States, backed by its allies, mostly European countries, seems more preoccupied by the "Fight Against Terror" and the Israeli-Palestinian conflict. Moreover, since the end of the Cold War, the Security Council seems to base its authority on Article 41 of the Charter of the United Nations, which advocates the imposition of economic and diplomatic sanctions in the form of embargo on travelling and on weapons to enforce its decisions.[34] Before the 9/11 (2001) World Trade Center (Twin Towers) & Pentagon attacks in America, many observers accused the Security Council of having imposed sanctions on mostly the South including Libya, Sudan and Zimbabwe, but not on the United States for violating the principle of non-aggression of the United Nations by invading a sovereign country, Iraq, after 9/11 on the pretext that Iraq was holding weapons of mass destruction. This incited many observers, especially Africans to consider the reform of the Security Council as strategically important and urgent for the parties who do not have a permanent seat in it, considering the many political, economic and diplomatic stakes it raised, vis-à-vis Africa's development; notwithstanding the fact that the United States, without obtaining the endorsement of the Security Council, bypassed UN to invade Iraq.[35]

---

[34] The Security Council may decide what measures not involving the use of armed force are to be employed to give effect to its decisions, and it may call upon the Members of the United Nations to apply such measures. These may include complete or partial interruption of economic relations and of rail, sea, air, postal, telegraphic, radio, and other means of communication, and the severance of diplomatic relations. (Article 41)

[35] The P-3 members of the Council (the US, France and Britain) have, without the endorsement of the United Nations Security Council, led multi-national military interventions, such as Kosovo in 1999 and Iraq in 2003; France neither supported nor participated in the Iraq intervention.

The reform of the Security Council

During the jubilee anniversary of the United Nations in 1995, the Heads of State and Government of its Member States adopted a declaration endorsing the idea of enlarging the Security Council. That confirmed the importance of the issue of the composition of the Council especially for developing countries. However, if the need for the democratisation of the UN through reforming the size, especially the number of permanent members, and functioning of the Security Council is evident, it seems difficult to find a satisfactory solution or even a departure. Firstly, will the enlargement of the Security Council solve the problem or create more problems, considering the history of the United Nations, and the nature of international politics and diplomacy? Should the Security Council be enlarged by creating new permanent seats, as the African Union had been advocating, or simply by increasing the non-permanent seats. How many new members should be added to the present composition? In short, on what criteria should the reform of the Security Council be based? Whatever the difficulties, the ways in which the reform should be undertaken given its importance, should be determined.

Africa and other parties seeking permanent membership are in favour of enlarging the Security Council by introducing new permanent seats with veto power, as well as new non-permanent seats to ensure a democratic representation in the United Nations Organisation. However, there are internal and external constraints, which must be resolved before any enlargement is effectively possible.

The first (internal) barrier to be lifted is to get the agreement of the General Assembly and individual members, especially the 5 permanent members, on a number of points. This procedure is described in Article 108 of the United Nations Charter, which states that:

Amendments to the present Charter shall come into force for all Members of the United Nations when they have been adopted by a vote of two thirds of the members of the General Assembly and ratified in accordance with their respective constitutional processes by two thirds of the Members of the United Nations, including all the permanent members of the Security Council.

The General Assembly must therefore first vote with a two-third majority; then Member States must ratify the decision in their national ratification procedures, including all the permanent members of the Security Council, meaning that any of the five permanent members can hamper the reform proposition. The final decision remains, therefore, in the hands of the permanent members of the Security Council. It is indeed this concentration of power in the hands of the permanent members of the Security Council that symbolises its lack of democracy from the perspective of the African Union. The second type of obstacle concerns international relations in the form of politics and diplomacy, which may delay or even obstruct the process. Firstly, there are divisions and divergence among the permanent members for the choice of countries for permanent seats, as well as rivalries amongst the candidates. The multiplicity of candidates for permanent seats and the political and military rivalry of some of the contending countries could jeopardise the proposed reform programme. For example, the disputes between India and Pakistan especially over Kashmir,[36] and

---

[36]The history of the Kashmir conflict which is an ongoing territorial dispute between India and Pakistan goes back to 1947, when both Pakistan and India got independence from the British. Kashmir has always been an independent territory. Until 1846; it was part of the Sikh Empire. In that year, the British defeated the Sikhs and sold Kashmir to Gulab Singh of Jammu under the Treaty of Amritsar. Gulab Singh, the Maharaja, signed a separate treaty with the British which gave him the status of an independent princely ruler of Kashmir. The roots of the conflict between the Kashmiri insurgents and the Indian Government are tied to a dispute over local autonomy. Democratic development was limited in Kashmir until the late 1970s and by 1988 many of the democratic

those between China and Japan, which date back to the period of Japanese Imperialism,[37] especially during the Second Sino-Japanese War and World War II, where some events and incidents have been described as an Asian Holocaust, citing Japanese war crimes and atrocities. As it is evident that the final decision lies in the hands of the permanent members of the Security Council, China can veto Japan's candidacy or any other's in Asia for a permanent seat, as it did in 1955 to block Mongolia's accession to membership of the United Nations. Thus, the reforms will not materialise as long as the permanent members of the Security Council do not genuinely rally to it. It is therefore important to study the position of each permanent member of the Security Council.

The United States has not overtly been hostile to the enlargement of the Security Council, in spite of their opinion that any UN reform must be gradual and progressive to be effective and not disrupt the functioning of the Organisation. According to Kristen Silverberg, Assistant Secretary of State of the United States for International Organisations from 2005 to 2008, "... the United States is in favour of the enlargement of the Security Council at an appropriate time, but [...] would like to see progress on other aspects of the reform of the United Nations, before moving on this issue."(droitpublic.net) For the United States then, the reform of the Security Council must be considered as part of a broader framework of reform of the United Nations. This means that the enlargement of the Security Council should not be considered uniquely at the expense of the other problems of the United Nations. Thus the United States welcomes the enlargement of the Security Council to

---

reforms provided by the Indian Government had been reversed and non-violent channels for expressing discontent were limited and caused a dramatic increase in support for insurgents advocating violent secession from India.

[37] Japanese imperialism refers to the ideology prevalent in the Empire of Japan that considered that militarism should dominate the social and political life of the nation, and that the force of the nation is the strength of the military.

increase its representation, but without the Council losing its effectiveness.

In September 1995 the United States' permanent representative to the working group on the enlargement of the Security Council threatened to use the United States veto against any proposal that would not include permanent memberships for Japan and Germany. (AG10418) The motivation behind the U.S. specific support for the candidacy of Japan and Germany is most probably based on the idea that the two countries are amongst the major economic powers and can therefore contribute more to financing UN military operations and especially to the resources of the Organisation. Japan and Germany have become the second and third largest contributors to the United Nations, 10.83 % and 7.14 % respectively more than France's 5.59 %, the United Kingdom of Great Britain and Northern Ireland's 5.17 %, and China's 5.14 %. (un.org) Russia is not among the top ten financial contributors to the Organisation. The United States' policy vis-à-vis the United Nations seems therefore to be strategically looking for a way of significantly supplementing its contribution to the Organisation's resources in the coming years. The overall position of the United States supports a reasonable increase in the number of members of the Council by a combination of permanent and non-permanent members to help enhance its effectiveness. It, however, believes that the new permanent members should be highly qualified to be able to deal with their immense tasks and responsibilities. The criteria amongst others for US were the country size, military capacity, contributions to UN peace-keeping missions and record on combating terrorism and weapon proliferation. (bloomberg.com)

Visibly, the North American point of view vis-à-vis the enlargement of the Security Council is based on the idea that the reform of the Security Council should be made to increase its representation, but without losing its effectiveness. Also, the status of permanent members should not only be linked with the simple notion of democracy and geographical representation, but also to a number of criteria, including the power and ability to provide a significant financial contribution to the maintenance and functioning of the Organisation, which is a critical position vis-à-vis the African Union's demand. For the United States, the composition of the Council should not exceed 24 members. In addition to Germany and Japan, the United States in 1997 declared its support to the candidacy of three developing countries for permanent seats on the Security Council, without clearly naming specific countries. (ibid) It has however disregarded the idea of granting a developing country the veto right. After Germany's opposition to the US invasion of Iraq in 2003, George W Bush's administration withdrew US support from Germany. Later the changes at the head of the two administrations enabled the two countries to restore a cordial relationship and the new German Chancellor, Angela Merkel, renewed German support for U.S. foreign policy, hence the renewal of U.S. support for Germany. The recent scandal over numerous revelations, originating principally from Edward Snowden showing the pervasive character of the US spying on its allies in Europe, including Germany, by the United States National Security Agency (NSA) in October 2013, and especially the phone tapping of the German Chancellor Angela Merkel's cell phone, which led to the expulsion of US intelligence agents from Germany in July 2014, however, will surely create more difficulties between the two parties to consequently affect US support for Germany's candidacy for a permanent seat in the Security Council. This confirms that US support for candidates for permanent seats in the Security Council is strategic and unstable.

The United States reaffirmed its support for the candidacy of Japan, when John Bolton, the U.S. ambassador to the United Nations (2005 to 2006) stated that "Japan would occupy a permanent seat as soon as possible." (ibid) In November 2010, the U.S. President, Mr. Barack Obama, during a State visit to India, declared:

> As two global leaders, the United States and India can partner for global security - especially as India serves on the Security Council over the next two years. Indeed, the just and sustainable international order that America seeks includes a United Nations that is efficient, effective, credible and legitimate. That is why I can say today in the years ahead, I look forward to a reformed UN security council that includes India as a permanent member. (whitehouse.gov)

However, the accession of Germany and Japan to permanent seats in the Security Council with veto power will exacerbate the inequality and democratic deficiency of the representation on the Council that the African Union and other parties are denouncing, because Europe already has three permanent members sitting in the Security Council. The accession of a fourth European country, especially a major economic power like Germany, or a second Asian country like Japan, also a major economic power, or India, an emerging economic power, would most likely not be welcomed by the African continent, which has not yet got a single permanent seat in the Security Council.

The People's Republic of China has supported the reform of the Security Council in terms of democracy and development. Its representative, Wang Guangya, during debates on reform of the United Nations, emphasised the idea that:

> The Security Council reform by any means is merely a small part of the UN reform [...] China is in favour of a necessary and rational reform of the Security Council, including increasing the number of its members, the improvement of its working methods [...] to increase its efficiency and strengthen its role. The global trend towards

democratization of international relations should be reflected in the Security Council, [...] developing countries, which account for over two thirds of the Member States, were under-represented in the Council. The enlargement of the Security Council should give priority to increasing the representation of developing countries in general and African countries in particular, and increase the chances of more countries, particularly small and medium countries, to participate in decision-making. (un.org)

By this statement, China considers the reform of the Security Council as necessary and rational, to increase the number of its members, improve its working methods, and increase its efficiency, thereby strengthening its role. However, like the United States, it considers the reform of the Security Council as only a part of the overall reform of the United Nations. According to China a comprehensive reform of the Organisation should begin in stages, starting with the least complicated matters to solve. China has supported the position of developing countries, but it is opposed to a premature vote on UN reforms. It believes that developing countries, which account for over two-thirds of the United Nations General Assembly, are under-represented in the Council. The enlargement of the Security Council should, therefore, according to China, give priority to developing countries, including African countries. This would increase the chances for developing countries to participate and be involved in a fair decision-making process in the Organisation in the areas of peace, security and socio-economic development. Like most of the permanent members of the United Nations, China thus recognises the need for a democratic representation, with the idea that developed countries are over-represented in the Security Council. It opposes the candidacy of the G4,[38] especially that

---

[38] The G4 comprises Brazil, Germany, India and Japan; they cooperated and made a joint bid for permanent seats on UN Security Council. The group's first motive is to collectively struggle for permanent seats on the Security Council.

of Japan; presumably because it does not want to compete with a second Asian country on the international scene, especially at the United Nations. Moreover we have seen that China and Japan have not completely reconciled their differences dating back to the Sino-Japanese Wars and World War II. The political motivation behind China's position is therefore most probably a way to protect its monopoly in the region as far as the United Nations is concerned. Also China's support for Africa could be interpreted in the perspective of clientelism as a way of getting more access to Africa's energy resources, especially oil, which is normally strategic.

The position of the United Kingdom concerning the reform of the Security Council is not very far from that of the United States, seemingly for traditional reasons. This is demonstrated by Britain's behaviour during votes on resolutions of the Security Council. However, the United Kingdom does not seem to have much fear about the coming of new permanent members into the Security Council, even with veto power, as its policies within the United Nations should not be much affected. The UK does not seem to have any particular concern about the weakening of its status on the international stage, given the specificity of its relationship with the United States. Former Foreign Secretary Jack Straw, in his address to the Assembly in September 2004, underlined Britain's position to be:

> …in favour of permanent membership for the G-4, as well as its support for permanent membership for Africa. The United Kingdom would, therefore, vote in favour of the G-4 proposal. But it should be clear that the extension of the veto beyond the current five permanent members was not a necessary feature of expanded permanent membership, nor would it be in the wider interests of the United Nations. (un.org)

Britain's ambassador to the United Nations, Sir Emyr

Jones Parry, at the General Assembly of 11 November 2005 declared that:

> The UK favoured UN reform, including enlarging the Security Council as a key element [...] for increasing the number of both permanent and non-permanent members, [...] an enlarged and strengthened Council would better represent the wider United Nations membership and be more capable of meeting the challenges of today's world. (ibid)

However, assigning a permanent seat to Zimbabwe especially under President Robert Mugabe, who has won his seventh term in office in the presidential election of August 2013, would be unacceptable to the United Kingdom due to Mugabe's land policy regarding white farmers in Zimbabwe.

France also expressed the view that the Security Council should better represent the Member States of the United Nations, to be capable of confronting the problems of international peace and security. During the Franco-British summits on the reform of the Security Council in March 2008 and July 2009, the two countries demonstrated their approval for an enlargement of the Security Council. In a joint statement in July 2009, they supported a "...pragmatic option of an interim reform that could include a new category of seats with a longer term than the current elected members. After this interim phase, these new seats could be changed into permanent seats."[39] (franceonu.org) France backs the candidature of G4 to which Germany, the principal old enemy of the Allies belongs, and that of Africa to a permanent seat. However, we have seen that the accession of Germany to the Security Council as a permanent member with veto power would aggravate the

---

[39]...option pragmatique d'une réforme intérimaire qui pourrait prévoir une nouvelle catégorie de sièges avec un mandat plus long que celui des membres actuellement élus. A l'issue de cette phase intérimaire, il pourrait être décidé de transformer ces nouveaux sièges en sièges permanents... (franceonu.org)

democratic deficiency and inequality, and might not even be suitable and beneficial to France from a geopolitical and strategic point of view and in terms of international relations, in spite of the existence of the European Union. Membership of the Security Council with all the rights that the present permanent members have, would, given its economic power, enable Germany to exert more weight of diplomacy than France and hence play a relatively major political role in the European Union and consequently benefit from greater recognition on the international scene. Germany, occupying a permanent seat, while its financial contribution to the United Nations is more important than that of France and the United Kingdom, would hold a more important position than these two countries in the international system. The status of a permanent member of the Security Council would hence give Germany more economic power, assign it a leading role in Europe, strengthen its status in international relations and diplomacy, and accordingly give it the status of a great power alongside the United States, to become one of the most important countries and leading role players in Europe. This undoubtedly would affect the status of France on the international scene, as well as the balance of power in Europe, which was the main reason for Britain's support for France's entrance into this prestigious Council. France would have little to gain individually from the granting of a permanent seat to Germany with veto power, yet it openly affirmed its support for the aspirations of the G4, of which Germany is part. Also during the visit of Prime Minister Manmohan Singh of India to France in September 2005, President Jacques Chirac reaffirmed France's support for India's candidature for a permanent seat on the Security Council. (lemonde.fr)

France also considers it essential that the African continent has its place on the Council. During the Summit of the African Union in Addis Ababa (Ethiopia) on January

30, 2011, the French President at that time, Mr. Nicolas Sarkozy, reaffirmed France's support for Africa, declaring:

> I have been convinced for a long time that Africa does not have its right place in international governance. So, as the President of the General Assembly of the United Nations and the Secretary General are here, I am asking them to reform the Security Council this year. Do not wait. France will support you. Do not make speeches, make decisions. Increase the number of members of the Security Council, to accord the billions of Africans the place to which they are entitled, and France will support you...[40] (franceonu.org)

Just recently, the new French President François Hollande declared on August 27, 2012: "I want to push forward the reform of the Security Council to allow new permanent as well as non-permanent members there."[41] (Franceonu.org)

Russia was initially relatively more cautious about the reform of the Security Council, but like the others it recognised the need for better representation on the Council, with the participation of influential developing countries. Russia also supports the idea that the role of the Security Council in conflict resolution should be strengthened, but it is opposed to an excessive enlargement that could affect its efficiency. According to Russia, the realities of international relations show that the Security Council should be opened to new permanent members, and these positions should not be occupied only by industrialised countries; developing

---

[40] Je suis convaincu depuis bien longtemps que l'Afrique n'a pas la place qu'il lui revient dans la gouvernance internationale. Alors, puisque le Président de l'Assemblée générale des Nations Unies est ici et que le Secrétaire général est ici, je leur dis : faites la réforme du Conseil de sécurité dès cette année. N'attendez pas. La France vous soutiendra. Ne faites pas un discours, prenez des décisions. Elargissez le nombre de membres du Conseil de sécurité, reconnaissez au milliard d'Africains la place à laquelle ils ont droit et la France vous soutiendra.... (franceonu.org)

[41] «Je souhaite faire avancer la réforme du Conseil de sécurité pour permettre à de nouveaux membres permanents comme non permanents d'y siéger.» (franceonu.org)

countries should also occupy permanent seats on the Security Council. However, Russia believes that any initiative to change the function or composition of the Security Council should be treated with caution. It has proposed the same number of seats as the United States of America, i.e. about twenty permanent and non-permanent seats all together. Just like the other permanent members, Russia believes that the goal of enlarging the Security Council is to strengthen its efficacy in its role of safeguarding international peace and security. However, it expressed its opposition to any proposal that would offer new members the same prerogatives as the current members, i.e. conferring the veto right on new members that, according to Russia, will be counter-productive and will build tension. (AG/10418)

Since the 1990s, the Russian Federation has had relatively less success due to the breaking away of many parts of the former U.S.S.R. to become independent. Internationally, it now relies more on its status as a permanent member of the Security Council than on its political, economic and/or military capacity, in spite of its nuclear power and its natural resources. Therefore the accession to permanent membership of emerging economic powers such as India and developed countries like Japan and Germany to the Security Council with veto power will most probably relegate Russia to a relatively inferior position on the international scene. Its relative weakness in the economic domain and the political instability it has experienced has marginalised it since the collapse of the Soviet Union. Consequently, it may delay any reform aimed at attributing new Security Council members veto power, which would exacerbate its relative marginalisation and weakness on the international scene. It is most probably for this reason that Russia supported the entry of developing countries, while opposing the attribution of veto power to new members. Hence ratification of an amendment of the Charter to enlarge the Security Council to include new permanent members by Russia seems not very likely.

We can see that overall, the five permanent members logically admit the necessity of a democratic and equitable representation of members of the United Nations on the Security Council, but it is also evident by their declarations that most of them are not straightforward on the issue and that there is an obvious lack of enthusiasm. England, France and Russia are opposed to conferring the veto right to new members, and the USA is against conferring it to developing countries.

The reform of the Security Council presents two concepts, namely democratisation or fairness, and effectiveness. The concept of fairness refers to the idea that all continents must in an equal and democratic manner serve on the Security Council. However, concerning efficiency, which refers to the Council functioning in the best possible way with the least waste of resources, efforts and time, it is important to see if the enlargement of the Security Council will make it more competent, since a fair representation cannot take place without increasing the number of permanent members. In other words, will the increase in the number of permanent seats of the Security Council with veto power make it more efficient or on the contrary weaken it? The current permanent members might fear or pretend that enlarging the Security Council with permanent members with veto power risks it being paralysed by frequent and abusive use of the veto, in other words, it could transform it into an arena of political and ideological battle, as was the case during the Cold War. The Security Council, being an executive body, should have the ability to meet quickly so as to take effective and concrete measures, and the increase in the permanent members would likely affect this capacity, as well as the effectiveness of the Council, especially during major crises.

There could be some reason in this point of view, because of the high probability of a selfish use of the veto in a Security Council, say with twenty five permanent members all with veto power, compared to the current five permanent members. However, the effectiveness of the Security Council has already been seriously damaged by the frequent and excessive use of the veto especially during the Cold War. The diminution of this misuse of the veto after the Cold War and the fear of the Security Council[42] being propelled to the same position might be justified, but if that occurs in an atmosphere of equality, democracy and legitimacy, according to the African Union's logical interpretation of the Charter of the United Nations, there is no reason to refuse the admission of new permanent members and to accord these members the veto right. The fear of lack of credibility, democracy and effectiveness of the Council is a constant fear, it has always existed and will always exist; that should therefore not prevent the enlargement of the Security Council. The enlargement of the Council should indeed strengthen its effectiveness and credibility, as it will be more representative, more democratic and more legitimate, thereby making its resolutions and the Council itself more accepted. This reasoning is relevant because the decisions of the Security Council were frequently challenged by Member States on the grounds of their lack of legitimacy, or because of their partiality.

Africa reasonably associates the legitimacy and democratisation of the Security Council with the continent's permanent membership of the Council with veto power, which should symbolise the institution of democracy in the Council and the end of Africa's continuing marginalisation, as the only continent not having a permanent seat in the Council. The position of the United States, which argued that the status of permanent seats in the Security Council should not only be linked to the simple notion of geographical representation and democracy, is critical to the

---

[42] Moreover the fear could be contained if all the permanent members constructively observe the provisions of the charter in dialogue and discipline.

position of Africa. However, this reasoning of the United States is faulty because the socio-political sense of representation refers basically, in most nations including the United States itself, to democracy and geography, with an effective mechanism of checks and balances. Member States will welcome United Nations' resolutions far more when they are made by an organism in which the whole world is represented with the same privileges and rights. If the African continent is not attributed at least one permanent seat with veto power on the Security Council like the current permanent members, the positive contribution that the United Nations has made to African reparation that we have underlined, will continue to be offset and residual. The proposal of reform of the Security Council that seeks to make it more broadly and equitably representative will result, according to the judgement of the African Union, in strengthening its representation, transparency and accountability, as well as its democratisation and the legitimacy of its decisions. This will also give the African Union its rightful and proper role in the international politico-economic system, as an important factor of African reparation. Also the reform should not be limited to increasing the number of permanent members with veto right, but it should equally include the improvement of the working methods of the Security Council and the United Nations in General. This will confirm the positive role that the United Nations is playing in African reparation.

Conclusion

The United Nations was established at the beginning of the 1940s to safeguard and promote international cooperation, peace and security, as a means of ensuring the safety, stability and development of the international socio-economic systems after the devastating effects of World War II in the 1940s. It contributed significantly to the attainment of independence for a large part of Africa, to the killing of apartheid and the decline of racism, as well as to the promotion of development on the entire African continent. However, its structures and functioning have been severely criticised for having contributed to, and even accelerated, the marginalisation of Sub-Saharan Africa. The operations of the United Nations do not tend to comply satisfactorily with the fundamental principles of equality and democracy that have been its raison d'être, consequently making Africa a victim.

The United Nations has enormously assisted Africa in its struggle for independence, but it has also, partly, contributed to its marginalisation, at least indirectly. The structure and functioning of the Organisation, especially its Security Council, have been unsuitable to Africa, and have even increased its marginalisation. The United Nation's Security Council, as the most important decision-making body of the Organisation, has the power to impose both economic and military sanctions on any Member State that poses a threat to international peace and security, and can intervene militarily in such countries. However, membership of this Council has been entrusted to only five nations with permanent seat and veto power, which are the guiding powers of the Allied force in World War II. This situation is not justifiably democratic; moreover the geopolitical situation of the world has changed enormously since then. Therefore today, 70 years after the UN was formed in the aftermath of World War II, the victors of the war hold all the cards. Consequently the composition of the Security

Council no longer reflects the realities of international relations. The veto power of the permanent members of the Security Council was strategically invented in 1945 as a presumably constructive apparatus for the UN to survive the dissensions that otherwise could have terribly affected its existence and threatened international peace. However, it prevented the Member States not represented in the Council from playing their rightful constructive role in the maintenance of international peace and security, and moreover, from reasonably and justifiably dealing with the affairs of the powers that sit on permanent seats in the Security Council. This veto power also affects the fundamental freedom and rights of Member States which do not have it, particularly African countries in the domain of international relations. In fact, Member States not on the council have considered it as not solving their problems.

Peace and security are matters that concern everyone, not just an elite group in the United Nations. Because the problems concern the majority of Member States, each Member State through representation should have a say in solving them. Africa was aware of its relegation within the United Nations and consequently all the injustice and marginalisation that accompany it, well back in the 1960s, when the OAU requested permanent seats in the Council. The absence of Africa as a permanent member of the Security Council because it was not part of the major architects of the Allied victory and the source of the creation of the UN, is not legitimate especially given the current configuration of the world. It has therefore become imperative to reformulate the composition of the Security Council, to find a new, more democratic arrangement for the United Nations to fulfil its essential functions, which is the maintenance of international peace and security in a legitimate manner, as the changes on the international scene require a balance between the various parts of the world. Given the geopolitical situation of the world today, the representation of the West, especially Western Europe is too much compared to that of other regions, especially Africa, which does not have a single permanent representative on the Council. Therefore the mechanism on which the UN works, especially the Security Council, no longer ensures the democratic participation of all regions. To ensure greater democracy, the power within the Organisation, which has a global socio-economic vocation, should not be concentrated in the hands of industrialised countries uniquely because they were at the origin of the victory that led to the formation of the Organisation. The enlargement of the Security Council is therefore a fundamental element in international relations today, without which the Security Council will continue to be less effective.

This is also important from the perspective of creating a new more constructive world order, and contributing to the reparation of the effects of slavery, Colonialism and apartheid in Africa. The current composition and functioning of the Security Council affect the process of reparation in Africa, because there is no way to rectify the situation when a world power sitting on a permanent seat in the Council is arbitrarily hostile to the policies of an African country, and when the interests of the African Union are at stake. Moreover, if the veto is to be continuously seen as a means of preventing tensions to escalate, all continental regions should democratically participate in the process of exercising the privilege.

But for Africa and others to become permanent members with veto power, the General Assembly must endorse it with a two-thirds majority, and then the amendment must be ratified by individual Member States and then finally be agreed upon by the actual permanent members of the Security Council, according to the provisions of Article 108 of the Charter of the United Nations. However, the position of the permanent members on the subject reveals their reluctance to share this veto right with potential members.

The contention of G4 may pose problems because of its controversial nature. The United States has supported the candidature of members of G4, because the economic power of the countries that form the group justify it. China has largely supported the reform for greater representation of developing countries, but has not been committed to an extension of the veto power to new members, owing particularly to its desire for Japan not to possess such a privilege. Russia has equally not been keen about the reform of the Council, due mainly to its relative economic and political weakness, thereby not having the desire to see developed and emerging countries be part of it, a situation that is liable to relegate its position on the international scene. For example China and Russia categorically opposed Japan's bid and presumably also that of India. In addition, India's candidature would surely upset Pakistan because of the enmity between the two countries over Kashmir, a problem created by Western colonisation. Even if Pakistan is not in a position to do much about it, they would surely try to lobby against it. A similar politico-military rivalry exists between China and Japan, meaning that China will most likely veto Japan's bid for a permanent seat. The French position, like that of the other permanent members, is however still ambiguous in relation to their willingness to sincerely support the reform of the Security Council. The overall position of the permanent members shows that they are not willing to share their veto power with new members of the Council.[43] There is also no indication yet that they genuinely support the candidacy of the African Union, despite the moral responsibility of Britain, France and USA in African reparation for their role in the Atlantic slave trade and/or Colonialism. Neither the UK nor France, nor the other members demonstrated a clear enough support for

---

[43] Russia has categorically demonstrated its opposition to the attribution of veto rights to new permanent members of the Security Council, and the USA has expressed opposition to attributing the veto right to developing countries.

Africa in its quest for permanent seats with veto rights.

Another difficulty for Africa is that the African Union, in seeking permanent seats has generally adopted a seemingly maximalist position because it has opted for an almost direct action visa-à-vis its request for permanent membership, demanding nothing less than two permanent seats with veto power as expressed in the Ezulwini Consensus. This rigid stance risks creating difficulties for the continent and might even hamper the possibility of other reforms that could favourably lead to a progressive acquisition of the veto right.

It is obvious that the United Nations has accomplished, at least partially, its primary objective, which is the maintenance of international peace and security. The Organisation has been valuable at times of tension and conflict between Member States, serving as a forum in which they settle their differences relatively peacefully. It can even be seen as the only viable alternative, so far, to international conflict and war. Through its Security Council, the Organisation has also constructively played a major role in conflict resolution and peace-keeping in Africa. The most recent examples are the Democratic Republic of Congo, Mali and the Central African Republic where the United Nations, in collaboration with the African Union and the Regional Economic Communities, successfully brought an end to the conflicts. However, considering the issue of representation and democratic legitimacy, increasing the permanent members of the UN Security Council should take into account a more equitable geographical distribution, even if, despite the lack of fair representation in the Council, the General Assembly of the United Nations continues to have a rather positive role and is an organ accessible to all for peaceful and progressive dialogue. The presence of all the continents in the Council will render it more efficient, democratic and legitimate.

The United Nations Organisation is not legitimately engaged in the maintenance of international peace and security, because the African continent is deprived of its rights of being democratically involved in it, and those countries in the council as permanent members with veto rights do not see the council as a vehicle for solving problems; they rather exercise their veto power strategically as an instrument to affirm their domination on non-veto wielding members of the United Nations.

Over 70 years of existence, this often bureaucratic organisation, which as we have seen had just 51 members when it was formed in 1945, surely has the ability to prevent conflict in the world; therefore, in a global sense, the UN is relatively relevant and therefore fit for purpose. However, its Security Council has not been able to live up to its functions, because it is not being democratically employed for the purpose that it was designed for, which has a global reflection on the general functioning and purpose of the United Nations. The reform of the Council is therefore urgently needed especially in the context of African reparation, but it is unlikely to happen soon.

Bibliography

Primary sources

Personal interviews

Personal interview, 20 June 2007.

Personal interview, 15 July 2007

Archives of the African Union

CIAS/PLEN.2/REV.2 / A – F CIAS/Plen.3 / A – C CIAS/RES.1/REV.1 / IAS/Res.1/Rev.1 / CIAS/Res.2 Resolution adopted by the first conference of independent African Heads of State and government held in Addis Ababa, Ethiopia, 22 – 25 May 1963.

AHG/Res. 1 (1) - AHG/Res. 24 (1) Resolution adopted by the first conference of independent African Heads of State and government held in Cairo, UAR, 17 - 21 July 1964.

AHG/Res. 25 (II) - AHG/Res. 45 (II) Resolution adopted by the second ordinary session of the Assembly of Heads of State and government held in Accra, Ghana 21 – 26 October 1965.

AHG/Res. 46 (III) - AHG/Res. 48 (III) Resolution adopted by the third ordinary session of the Assembly of Heads of State and government held in Addis Ababa, Ethiopia, 5 - 9 November 1966.

AHG/Res. 104 (XIX) Resolution on Western Sahara, assembly of Heads of State and government, Nineteenth Ordinary Session 6 – 12 June 1983 Addis Ababa, Ethiopia.

AHG/Res. 111 (XIX) Resolution on the policy of destabilisation by racist South African regime against Southern African Independent States, Assembly of Heads of State and government, Nineteenth Ordinary Session 6 – 12 June 1983 Addis Ababa, Ethiopia.

AHG/Res. 112 (XIX) Resolution on South Africa, assembly of Heads of State and government, Nineteenth Ordinary Session 6 – 12 June 1983 Addis Ababa, Ethiopia.

AHG/Res. 113 (XIX) Resolution on the African candidatures to international organisations, Assembly of Heads of State and government, Nineteenth Ordinary Session 6 – 12 June 1983 Addis Ababa, Ethiopia.

AHG/Res. 115 (XIX) Resolution on the Lagos Plan of Action and the Final Act of Lagos, Assembly of Heads of State and government, Nineteenth Ordinary Session 6 – 12 June 1983 Addis Ababa, Ethiopia.

AHG/Res.130 (XIX) Resolution on the Establishment of a Special Fund for Africa, Assembly of Heads of State and government, Twentieth Ordinary Session 12 – 15 November 1984 Addis Ababa, Ethiopia.

AHG/Res.131 (XIX) Resolution on the Inter-African Economic Co-operation and Integration, Assembly of Heads of State and government, Twentieth Ordinary Session 12 – 15 November 1984 Addis Ababa, Ethiopia.

AHG/Res.190 (XXVI) Resolution on the Establishment of the African Economic Community, Assembly of Heads of State and government, Twenty-sixth Ordinary Session 9 – 11 July 1990 Addis Ababa, Ethiopia.

AHG/Res.198 (XXVI) Resolution on the African Commission on Human and Peoples' Rights, Assembly of Heads of State and government, Twenty-sixth Ordinary Session 9 – 11 July 1990 Addis Ababa, Ethiopia.

AHG/Decl.1. (XXVIII) Decision on a Mechanism for Conflict Prevention, Management and Resolution, Assembly of Heads of State and government, Twenty-eighth Ordinary Session 29 June – 1 July 1992.

Assembly/AU/Dec.95 (VI) Decision on the Statutes of the African Academy of Languages (ACALAN).

Decision CM/Dec. 613 (LXXIV) of Lusaka related to the establishment of the African Academy of Languages.

AHG/Decl.2 (XXXVI) Lome Declaration, Assembly of Heads of State and government, Thirty-Sixth Ordinary Session/Fourth Ordinary Session of the African Economic Community 10-12 July, 2000 Lome, Togo.

AHG/Decl.5 (XXXVI) Declaration on the Framework for an OAU response to unconstitutional changes of government, Assembly of Heads of State and government, Thirty-Sixth Ordinary Session/Fourth Ordinary Session of the African Economic Community 10-12 July, 2000 Lome, Togo.

AHG/Dec.143 (XXXVI) Decision on the establishment of the African Union and the Pan-African Parliament, Assembly of Heads of State and government, Thirty-Sixth Ordinary Session/Fourth Ordinary Session of the African Economic Community 10-12 July, 2000 Lome, Togo.

AHG/Dec.150 (XXXVI) Decision on unconstitutional changes of government in Africa - CM/2166 (LXXII) Assembly of Heads of State and government, Thirty-Sixth Ordinary Session/Fourth Ordinary Session of the African Economic Community 10-12 July, 2000 Lome, Togo.

AHG/Dec.1 (XXXVII) Decision on the Implementation of the Sirte Summit Decision on the African Union, Assembly of Heads of State and government, Thirty-seventh Ordinary Session/Fifth Ordinary Session of the AEC 9 – 11 July, 2001 Lusaka, Zambia.

AHG/Decl.1 (XXXVII) Declaration on the New Common Initiative (MAP and OMEGA), Assembly of Heads of State and government, Thirty-seventh Ordinary Session/Fifth Ordinary Session of the AEC 9 – 11 July, 2001 Lusaka, Zambia.

Assembly/AU/Dec.17 (II) Decision on the Protocol to the Treaty Establishing the African Economic Community Relating to the Pan-African Parliament, Assembly of the African Union, Second Ordinary Session 10 - 12 July 2003 Maputo, Mozambique.

Ext/Assembly/AU/Dec.2 (II) Decision on a Non-aggression and common defence pact, Assembly of the African Union, 2nd Extraordinary Session 27 - 28 February 2004 Sirte, Libya.

Assembly/AU/Dec.83 (V) Decision on the Merger of the African Court on Human and Peoples' Rights and the Court of Justice of the African Union – (Doc. Assembly/AU/6 (V)), Assembly of the African Union, Fifth Ordinary Session 4 – 5 July 2005 Sirte, Libya.

Assembly/AU/Decl. 2 (V) Sirte Declaration on the Reform of the United Nations, Assembly of the African Union, Fifth Ordinary Session 4 – 5 July 2005 Sirte, Libya.

Assembly/AU/Resolution.1 (V) Resolution on the United Nations Reform: Security Council Assembly of the African Union, Fifth Ordinary Session 4 – 5 July 2005 Sirte, Libya.

Assembly/AU/Dec.166 (IX) Decision on the Protocol on Relations between the African Union and the Regional Economic Communities (RECs) - Doc. EX.CL/348 (IX), Assembly of the African Union, Ninth Ordinary Council 1 – 3 July 2007 Accra, Ghana.

OAU AHG/decl3 (XXXIII) Harare Declaration of the Assembly of Heads of State and Government of the OAU on the Reform of the UN Security Council Thirty-third Ordinary Session 2 – 4 June 1997 Harare, Zimbabwe.

Ext/EX.CL/2 (VII) The Common African Position on the Proposed Reform of the United Nations: *"The Ezulwini Consensus"* Executive Council, 7th Extraordinary Session 7- 8 March 2005, Addis Ababa, Ethiopia.

Organisation of African Unity. OAU Charter. 25 May 1963, Addis Ababa, Ethiopia.

African Union. Constitutive Act of the African Union, 11 JULY, 2000, Lome, Togo.

Archives of the United Nations Organisation

UN. ECOSOC Resolution 2002/1 Ad hoc advisory group on African countries emerging from conflict 23rd plenary meeting, 15 July 2002.

UNTS XVI, United Nations, Charter of the United Nations, 1945, 1 UNTS XVI.

AG/10418) Rapport de débat sur l'élargissement du Conseil à l'Assemblée générale, 47ᶜ& 48ᵉ séances plénières, le 11 novembre 2005.

A/CONF.189/12. Report of the World Conference against Racism, Racial Discrimination, Xenophobia and Related Intolerance, Durban, 31 August- 8 September 2001.

S/RES/462 (1980) International peace and security, 9 January 1980.

S/RES/308 (1972) Request of the Organization of African Unity concerning the holding of meetings of the Security Council in an African Capital (General Assembly Resolution 2863 (XXVI), para. 2), 19 January 1972.

S/RES/311 (1972) The Question of race conflict in South Africa resulting from the policies of apartheid of the Government of the Republic of South Africa, 4 February 1972.

RES/190(1964) Question relating to the policies of apartheid of the Government of the Republic of South Africa. Resolution 190 (1964) Adopted by the Security Council on 9 June 1964.

S/RES/110 (1955) Question of reviewing the Charter of the UN Resolution of 14 December 1955 (s/3509)

S/RES/1631 (2005) Cooperation between the United Nations and regional organizations in maintaining international peace and security, Resolution 1631 (2005) Resolution 1631 (2005) Adopted by the Security Council at its 5282nd meeting, on 17 October 2005.

S/RES/1625 (2005) Threats to international peace and security (Security Council Summit 2005), Resolution 1625 (2005) Adopted by the Security Council at its 5261st meeting, on 14 September 2005.

S/RES/1624 (2005) Threats to international peace and security (Security Council Summit 2005), Resolution 1624 (2005) Adopted by the Security Council at its 5261st meeting, on 14 September 2005.

S/RES/1631 (2005) Cooperation between the United Nations and regional organizations in maintaining international peace and security, Resolution 1631 (2005) Adopted by the Security Council at its 5282nd meeting, on 17 October 2005.

S/RES/1318 (2000) Effective role for the Security Council in the maintenance of international peace and security, particularly in Africa,

Resolution 1318 (2000) Adopted by the Security Council at its 4194th meeting, on 7 September 2000.

S/RES/919 (1994) South Africa Resolution 919 (1994) Adopted by the Security Council at its 3379th meeting, 25 May 1994.

S/RES/462 (1980) UN Security Council, Security Council Resolution 462 (1980) Adopted by the Security Council at its 2190th meeting, on 9 January 1980.

Resolution 2002/1 ECOSOC Ad hoc advisory group on African countries emerging from conflict 23rd plenary meeting, 15 July 2002.

Archives of the International Monetary Fund.

The International Monetary Fund. *World economic outlook: a survey by the staff of the International Monetary Fund.* Washington, D.C.: The International Monetary Fund, 1980.

International Monetary Fund. *World Economic Outlook (WEO), International Monetary Fund* Washington, D.C.: The International Monetary Fund, September 2006.

International Monetary Fund. *Regional economic outlook: Sub-Saharan Africa -* Washington, D.C.: International Monetary Fund, May 2006.

International Monetary Fund. *Integrating Poor Countries into the World Trading System* Washington, D.C: International Monetary Fund, April 2006.

International Monetary Fund. *Promoting Growth in Sub-Saharan Africa: Learning What Works,* Washington, D.C: International Monetary Fund, 2000.

The International Monetary Fund, the United Nations, the World Bank, and the Organisation for Economic Co-operation and Development. *A Better World for All Progress towards the international development goals,* Washington, D.C.: International Monetary Fund, 2000.

IMF, Articles of Agreement of the International Monetary Fund, Bretton Woods, New Hampshire, July 22, 1944.

Archives of the World Bank Group

World Bank. World Development Report 2005: A Better Investment Climate for Everyone, Washington, D.C.: World Bank, September 2004.

World Bank. World Development Report 2002: Building Institutions for Markets. Washington, D.C.: World Bank, September 2001.

World Bank. African Development Indicators 2005: From the World Bank Africa Database. Washington, D.C.: World Bank, July 2005.

World Bank. African Development Indicators 2004: Drawn from the World Bank Africa Database. Washington, D.C.: World Bank,

March 2004.

World Bank. Africa Development Indicators 2006: From the World Bank Africa Database. Washington, D.C.: World Bank, September 2006,

World Bank. The Uruguay Round: Widening and deepening the world trading system, Washington, D.C.: World Bank, October 1995.

The World Bank, IBRD Articles of Agreement (as amended effective June 27, 2012

World Bank. World Development Report 2003: Sustainable Development in a Dynamic World: Transforming Institutions, Growth, and Quality of Life August 2002, Oxford University Press.

Archives of the World Trade Organisation.

WT/MIN (01)/DEC/1 DOHA WTO Ministerial 2001: Ministerial Declaration. WT/MIN (01)/DEC/1 Adopted in Doha, 14 November 2001.

WT/MIN (01)/DEC/2 Declaration on the TRIPS Agreement and Public Health, Ministerial Conference, Fourth Session, Doha, 9 - 14 November 2001.

WTO. Uruguay Round Agreement, Marrakesh Declaration of 15 April 1994,

WT/MIN (13)/DEC Bali Ministerial Declaration and decisions adopted on 7 December 2013. WT/MIN (13)/31WT/L/906. Trips non-violation and situation complaints Ministerial Decision of 7 December 2013.

WT/MIN (13)/34WT/L/909 Aid for trade Ministerial Decision of 7 December 2013. WT/MIN (13)/35WT/L/910 Trade and Transfer of Technology, Ministerial Decision of 7 December 2013.

WT/MIN (13)/36WT/L/911 Agreement on trade and facilitation Ministerial Decision of 7 December 2013.

WT/MIN (13)/39WT/L/914 Understanding on tariff rate quota administration provisions of agricultural products, as defined in article 2 of the agreement on agriculture Ministerial Decision of 7 December 2013.

The General Agreement on Tariffs and Trade (GATT 1947)

Secondary sources

Books

A.

Ashcroft, Bill, Gareth Griffiths, and Helen Tiffin, ed. *Post-Colonial Studies*

Reader. London: Routledge, 1995.

Ayandele, E.A. *African Historical Studies*, United Kingdom, Routledge, 1979

B.

Boahen, A. Adu, dir. *Histoire générale de l'Afrique, volume VII* : L'Afrique sous domination coloniale, 1880-1935, Paris : UNESCO, 1987.

Boahen, A. Adu. *African Perspectives on Colonialism.* Baltimore: Johns Hopkins University Press, 1989.

Budhoo, Davidson. ed Kevin Danaher, *IMF / World Bank Wreak Havoc on Third World*, USA, South End Press, 1994.

Burke, Edmund. 2000. *On Empire, Liberty and Reform: Speeches and Letters.* Ed. David Bromwich. New Haven: Yale University Press.

Bute, E L, Harmer, H J P. *The Black Handbook: The People, History and Politics of African Diaspora.* London: Cassell, 1997.

C.

Ceesay, Amadou, ed. *Africa and Europe: from partition to independence or dependence.* London: Croom Helm, cop, 1986.

Centre for Conflict Resolution. *Africa, South Africa, and the United Nations' Security Architecture. Policy Advisory Group Seminar Report*, Cape Town: CCR, 2013.

Chinweizu, Onwuchekwa Jemie, Ihechukwu Madubuike. *Toward the Decolonization of African Literature.* Washington, D.C.: Howard University Press, 1983.

Connah, Graham. *African civilisations: pre-colonial cities and states in tropical Africa, an archaelogical perspective.* Cambridge: Cambridge *University Press, 1987.*

Cornevin, Robert. Histoire de l'Afrique: colonisation, décolonisation, indépendence. Paris : Payot, 1975.

D.

Dampha Lang Fafa. *Nationalism and Reparation in West Africa.* Paris: L'Harmattan, 2013.

Davidson, Basil. *Africa in modern history: the search for a new society.* London: Allen Lane, 1978.

Davidson, Basil. *The growth of African civilisation: a study of West Africa (1000-1800).* London: Longman, 1965.

Dickson, A Mungazi. *The Mind of Black Africa.* Connecticut: Westport, 1996.

Dingnan, Peter. *The United States and Africa: a history.* Cambridge:

Cambridge University Press, 1984.

Durgnan, Grann, Henry Lewis, Peter. *Colonialism in Africa: 1870-1960*. Cambridge: Cambridge University Press, 1969-1975. 5 Vol.

F.

Fage, Cliveret, John Donnelly, Rolland. *The Cambridge History of Africa*. Cambridge, London, New York, NY: Cambridge University Press, 1975.

Fanon Frantz. *Les damnés de la terre*, Paris : Éditions la Découverte, 1968.

Fanon, Frantz. *Peau Noire Masques Blancs*, Paris : Seuil, 1968.

Ferro, Marc ed. *Le livre noire du colonialisme XVIe – XXIe siècle : de l'extermination à la repentance*, Paris, éditions Robert Laffont, 2003.

Fleurence, Olivier. *La Réforme du Conseil de Sécurité : l'État du débat depuis la fin de la Guerre Froide*. Bruxelles, Établissements Émile Bruylant, 2000.

G.

Gann L H, Duignan Peter. *Colonialism in Africa 1870 – 1960* Volumes 1 and 2, New York, Cambridge University Press, 1969.

Gandhi, Leela. *Postcolonial Theory: A Critical Introduction*. New York: Columbia University Press, 1988.

Gordon, April A. and Donald L. Gordon, eds. *Understanding Contemporary Africa*. 2nd ed. Boulder, CO: Lynne Rienner Publishers, 1996.

H.

Hargreaves, John D. *Decolonization in Africa*, London: Longman Group UK. 1990.

Huntington, Samuel P. *Political Order in Changing Society*. New Haven and London, Yale University Press, 1968.

K.

Kennedy, Paul. *The Rise and fall of Great Powers*, London: Fontana Press, 1988.

Kitchen, Lexington, Helen, Mass, ed. *Africa: from mystery to maze*. Toronto: Lexington Books, 1978.

Killingray, David. *Africa and the Second World War*. London: Macmillan, 1986.

Kent, John. *The Internalization of Colonialism: Britain, France and Black Africa*. 1939-1956. Oxford: Oxford University Press, 1992.

King, Martin Luther Jr. *Stride Toward Freedom*, New York: Harper and Row, 1958.

L.

Lancaster, Carol. *So Much To Do, So Little Done*, Chicago: University of Chicago Press, 1999.

Legum, Colin. *Africa; a Handbook to the Continent*. New York: Praeger, 1962.

Loomba, Ania. *Colonialismpostcolonialism*. London, New York: Routledge, 1998.

Lynn, Martin. *Commerce and Economic Change in West Africa: the palm oil trade in the nineteenth century*. Cambridge: Cambridge University Press, 1997.

Lugan, Bernard. *Afrique: de la colonisation philanthropique à la recolonisation humanitaire*, Paris : Christian de Bartillat, 1995.

N.

Ndegwa, Philip. *Africa's Development Crisis*. London: Heinemann, 1988.

Ngugi wa Thiong'o. *Decolonising the Mind: The Politics of Language in African Literature*. London: J. Currey ; Portsmouth, N.H. : Heinemann, 1986.

Ngugi wa Thiong'o. *Moving the Centre: The Struggle for Cultural Freedoms*. London: J. Currey; Portsmouth, N.H.: Heinemann, 1993. .

Nkurumah, Kwame. *Towards Colonial Freedom: Africa in the struggle against world imperialism*. London: Panaf, 1979.

Nkurumah, Kwame. *Class Struggle in Africa*. London: Panaf, 1970.

Nkrumah, Kwame. *Neo-Colonialism: The Last Stage of Imperialism*, London: Heinemann, 1965.

Nkrumah, Kwame. *Challenge of the Congo. A Case Study of Foreign Pressures in an Independent State*, London: Panaf, 1966.

Nkrumah, Kwame. *Handbook of Revolutionary Warfare*, London: Panaf, 1968.

Nkrumah, Kwame. *Revolutionary Path*, London: Panaf, 1973.

O.

Oliver, Roland Anthony. *Africa in the Iron Age: C. 500 BC to AD 1400*. Cambridge, London, New York: Cambridge University Press, 1975.

Omer-Cooper J D. *The Making of Modern Africa*. New York: Humanities Press, 1968.

P.

Pitts, Jennifer. *A Turn Toward Empire: The Rise of Imperial Liberalism in Britain and France*. Princeton and Oxford: Princeton University Press, 2005.

R.

Ravenhill, John. *Africa in Economic Crisis*. London: Macmillan, 1986.

Reader, John. *Africa: A Biography of the Continent*. London: Hamish Hamilton, 1997, 840p.

Ricardo, David, *On the Principles of Political Economy and Taxation, 3rd edition*, London: John Murray, 1821.

Rodney, Walter. *How Europe Underdeveloped Africa*, Washington D.C.: Howard University Press, 1982.

S.

Shepherd, George W. Ed. Ved P. Nanda, George W. Shepherd, and Eileen McCarthy-Arnolds. *The African Right to Development and Adjustment: World Policy and the Debt Crisis*. Westport, CT: Greenwood Press, 1993.

T.

Thornton, John L. *Africa and Africans in the making of the Atlantic world: 1400-1800* 2nd ed. Cambridge, MA: Cambridge University Press, 1998.

Periodicals

Beck, Linda J., Senegal's "Patrimonial Democrats: Incremental Reform and Obstacles to the Consolidation of Democracy", *Canadian Journal Of African Studies*, Vol. 31, no1, (1997): 25.

Colette, Elise. "L'Afrique est une priorité", *Jeune Afrique l'intelligent*, n° 2198.43e année, (février – mars 2003) : 64.

Constantin, F. Constantin, B., "Perspectives africaines et bouleversements internationaux", *Politique Africaine, "l'Afrique autrement", n°39 (février 1990) :* 59.

Lucien Manokou, "L'Afrique et le Conseil de Sécurité de l'ONU (1946-1990)." *Guerres mondiales et conflits contemporains*, Paris, n° 196, décembre 1999 : 10.

Maja, Steven. "Distilling the vision of an African Union. " *Southern African Political & Economic Monthly (SAPEM)* Vol.14, N° 6, (2001): 5-6.

Manima, Norah. "Conflits africains: le lourd tribute économique", *La nouvelle Afrique*, n°6 (février – mars 2003): 42-45.

Web pages

ACALAN, "Terms of Reference for the harmonisation of the Fulfulde, Hausa and Mandenkan Vehicular Cross-border Languages, 14-16 July 2010." 10 Feb. 2013. <http://www.acalan.org/eng/accueil/accueil.php>

Apollos O. Nwauwa. "Concepts of Democracy and Democratization in Africa Revisited." *Paper presented at the Fourth Annual Kent State University Symposium on Democracy* 15 Aug. 2013.
<http://upress.kent.edu/Nieman/Concepts_of_Democracy.htm>
Bureau, Jean-Christophe, Decreux, Yvan, Gohin, Alexandre. "La libéralisation des échanges agricoles dans le cadre de l'OMC: impact économique." 15 Sept. 2013.
<http://www.insee.fr/fr/ffc/docs_ffc/ref/agrifra07k.pdf)>.
Driscoll, David D. "The IMF and the World Bank: How Do They Differ?" 12 June 2013.
<https://www.imf.org/external/pubs/ft/exrp/differ/differ.htm>
Bubulle, "Commentaire CIJ, essais nucléaires 1974." 10 Oct. 2013.
<http://www.juriste-en-herbe.com/droit-international-public/270-commentaire-cij-essais-nucleaires-1974>.
Le Droit suisse. "Droit International Public: L'affaire Nicaragua-USA." 05 Feb. 2013. <http://www.format-prod.com/droit-etudiants/dip-usa-nicaragua.html>.
UNESCO. "Bureau de l'UNESCO à Dakar." 13 May 2013.
<http://www.unesco.org/new/fr/dakar/about-this-office/>.
Houtart, François. "L'échec des politiques d'ajustement structurel de la Banque mondiale par (mai 2002) 02 Nov. 2013.
<http://www.cetri.be/spip.php?article420>
IDA, "ABCs of IDA—Thematic and Country Results." 10 Jan. 2014.
<http://www.worldbank.org/ida/ida_abc.html>
Malingumu Syosyo, Crispin. "Les interventions des institutions de Bretton Woods en Afrique : contraintes et limites. " 15 Jan. 2014.
<http://www.congoforum.be/fr/economiedetail.asp?subitem=31&id=23917&economie=selected>.
Defarges, Philippe Moreau. "La Reforme de l'ONU ? Obsedante et Impossible." 12 Feb. 2014. <http://www.afri-ct.org/IMG/pdf/67_Moreau_Defarges.pdf>.
Lecoutre, Delphine. "Des voix du Sud au Conseil de sécurité : L'Afrique et la réforme des Nations unies." juillet 2005. 18 Feb. 2014.
<http://www.monde-diplomatique.fr/2005/07/LECOUTRE/12441>.
Ramdoo, Isabelle. "9th WTO Ministerial in Bali: Trade deal struck, but what implications for geopolitics?" 06 Feb. 2014.
<http://www.ecdpm-talkingpoints.org/9th-wto-ministerial-in-bali-trade-deal-struck-but-what-implications-for-geopolitics/>.
Kanyimbo, Patrick, Calvin, Manduna. "Trade facilitation in the Bali Package: What's in it for Africa?" 06 Dec. 2013.
<http://www.afdb.org/en/blogs/integrating-africa/post/trade-

facilitation-in-the-bali-package-whats-in-it-for-africa-12698/>

"La France à l'ONU, Représentation permanent de la France auprès des Nations Unies à New York : La Réforme du Conseil de Sécurité des Nations Unies" 06 Aug. 2013. <http://www.franceonu.org/la-france-a-l-onu/dossiers-thematiques/reforme-de-l-onu/la-reforme-du-conseil-de-securite/article/la-reforme-du-conseil-de-securite>.

"Remarks by the President to the Joint Session of the Indian Parliament in New Delhi, India Parliament House, New Delhi, India." 08 Nov. 2010. <http://www.whitehouse.gov/the-press-office/2010/11/08/remarks-president-joint-session-indian-parliament-new-delhi-india>.

"The Common Agricultural Policy: A partnership between Europe and Farmers." 10 Nov. 2013. <http://ec.europa.eu/agriculture/cap-overview/2012_en.pdf>.

Georges-Henri Soutou, "La France et la creéation de l'ONU 1944-1946." 12 Aug. 2013. <http://www.diplomatie.gouv.fr/fr/IMG/pdf/ONU_gh_soutou.pdf>.

Nations Unies. "L'Assemblée Générale Débat de la Réforme du Conseil de Sécurité, Assemblée générale, 47e & 48e séances plénières, matin & après-midi." 20 Dec. 2013. <http://www.un.org/News/fr-press/docs/2005/AG10418.doc.htm>.

United Nations. "Remarks by Senator Jesse Helms to the United Nations Security Council." 10 Dec. 2013. <http://www.derechos.org/nizkor/impu/tpi/helms2.html>.

OMC. "Structure, fonctionnement, buts. 10 Aug. 2013. <http://perso.fundp.ac.be/~cedes6/f5/gr4/Cb_OMC_strct_fonct_buts.htm>.

The World Bank. "The World Bank's First Loan, May 9, 1947." 02 Feb 2014. <http://web.worldbank.org/WBSITE/EXTERNAL/EXTABOUTUS/EXTARCHIVES/0,,contentMDK:20035704~pagePK:36726~piPK:36092~menuPK:56273~theSitePK:29506,00.html>.

Socialist alternative. "Part I: The IMF, the World Bank, and the Global Economy." 15 Feb. 2014. <http://www.socialistalternative.org/publications/imfwb/>.

United Nations. "China supports UN Security Council reform, November 9, 2010." <http://www.un.org/News/Press/docs/2005/ga10368.doc.htm>.

WTO. "Documents from the negotiating chairs, 21 April 2011." 10 Jan. 2014. <http://www.wto.org/english/tratop_e/dda_e/chair_texts11_e/chair_texts11_e.htm>.

UNDP. "The United Nations Development Programme in Africa." 29 Dec. 2013. <http://www.africa.undp.org/rba/en/home.html>.

United Nations. "UN, ECOSOC MEMBERS." 10 Jan. 2014. <http://www.un.org/en/ecosoc/about/members.shtml>.

WTO. "The Doha Round." 15 Feb. 2014. <http://www.wto.org/english/tratop_e/dda_e/dda_e.htm>.

Féderation Internationale des Organisations de Travailleurs de la Metallurgie. "Les propositions OMC NAMA sont mauvaises pour le développement." 02 Jan. 2014. <http://www.imfmetal.org/index.cfm?c=16364&l=5>.

Laverie, Cedric. "La cohérence de la double conditionnalité des institutions de Bretton Woods, *Université Paris X - D.E.A. de Droit des Relations Economiques Internationales et Communautaires 2001.* 05 Dec. 2013. <http://www.memoireonline.com/08/08/1499/m_coherence-double-conditionnalite-institutions-bretton-woods4.html>.

United Nations. "Role of the General Assembly." 16 Nov. 2013. < https://www.un.org/en/peacekeeping/operations/rolega.shtml>

United Nations. "Role of the General Assembly." 15 Jan. 2013. <https://www.un.org/en/peacekeeping/operations/rolega.shtml

"The Common Agricultural Policy: A partnership between Europe and Farmers." 05 Dec. 2013. <http://ec.europa.eu/agriculture/cap-overview/2012_en.pdf

IMF. "At a Glance - China and the IMF" 10 Jan. 2014. <https://www.imf.org/external/country/chn/rr/glance.htm>

Nations Unies. "Groupes consultatifs spéciaux pour les pays africains qui sortent d'un conflit. " 05 Dec. 2013. <http://www.un.org/fr/ecosoc/adhocmech/conflict.shtml>.

Davison Budhoo. "Third world traveller, IMF/World Bank Wreak Havoc on Third World." 16 Nov. 2013. <http://www.thirdworldtraveler.com/IMF_WB/Budhoo_50YIE.html>.

Zacharia ,Janine. "U.S. Calls for Two More Permanent UN Council Seats." 08 Dec. 2013. <http://www.bloomberg.com/apps/news?pid=newsarchive&sid=aFdg w208I7jc>.

Nations Unies. "UNCTAD/SDTE/ECB/2005/1 Report: United Nations Conference on Trade and Development." Geneva, 31 Oct 2005. 20 Feb. 2014. <http://unctad.org/en/Docs/sdteecb20051overview_en.pdf>

ECOFIN FINANCE. "IFC : un record de 4 milliards $ d'investissements en Afrique subsaharienne." 20 Feb. 2014. <http://www.agenceecofin.com/investissement/3008-6451-ifc-un-

record-de-4-milliards-d-investissements-en-afrique-subsaharienne>.

Online Newspapers

Bobin, Frédéric. "Les BRICS haussent le ton sur la réforme de la Banque Mondiale et du FMI." *Le Monde*, 30 mars 2012. 10 Jan. 2013. <http://www.lemonde.fr/international/article/2012/03/30/les-brics-haussent-le-ton-sur-la-reforme-de-la-banque-mondiale-et-du-fmi_1678145_3210.html>.

Geneste, Alexandra. "Les Nations unies appellent la France à "décoloniser" la Polynésie", *Le Monde*, 18 mai, 2013. 02 Feb. 2013. <http://www.lemonde.fr/international/article/2013/05/18/les-nations-unies-appellent-la-france-a-decoloniser-la-polynesie_3316116_3210.html>.

Grunberg, Isabelle. "Que faire du Fonds monétaire international ? " *Le Monde diplomatique*, sept. 2000. 15 Jan. 2014. <http://www.monde-diplomatique.fr/2000/09/GRUNBERG/14172>.

Mbaye, Sanou. "En finir avec la dépendance : Souhaitable union des économies africaines," *Le Monde diplomatique*, septembre 1995. 13 Sept. 2012. <http://www.monde-diplomatique.fr/1995/09/MBAYE/1731>.

Lacouture, Jean. "Bandung ou la fin de l'ère coloniale." avril 2005. 25 Jul. 2012.
<http://www.monde-diplomatique.fr/2005/04/LACOUTURE/12062>

La Croix, "La résolution 2085 de l'ONU sur le Mali." *La Croix,* 14 Jan 2013. 16 Jan. 2014. <http://www.la-croix.com/Actualite/Monde/La-resolution-2085-de-l-ONU-sur-le-Mali-_NG_-2013-01-14-898950>.

Pacific Magazine, "REGION: Cook Islands puts New Zealand citizenship first", *Pacific Magazine*, 14 June 2001. 20 Feb. 2014.

Stiglitz, Joseph. "The Insider: What I Learnt at the World Economic Crisis." *The New Republic,* Washington DC, 17 April 2000. 03 Dec. 2013.
<http://sandovalhernandezj.people.cofc.edu/index_files/egl_20.pdf>.

Le Monde. "L'Inde et la France relancent leur partenariat stratégique." *Le Monde.fr avec AFP et Reuters,* 12 sept. 2005. 26 Feb. 2014. <http://www.lemonde.fr/asie-pacifique/article/2005/09/12/de-retour-aux-affaires-m-chirac-relance-le-partenariat-strategique-entre-l-inde-et-la-france_688394_3216.html>.

Robinson, Mary, "Africa Needs Fair Trade, Not Charity." *Yale Global,* 23 Aug 2005. 18 Jan. 2014. <http://yaleglobal.yale.edu/content/africa-needs-fair-trade-not-charity-0>

Joseph Stiglitz. "The Insider: What I Learnt at the World Economic Crisis", *The New Republic*, Washington DC, 17 April 2000. 16 Aug. 2013. <http://sandovalhernandezj.people.cofc.edu/index_files/egl_20.pdf>.

Libération. "Jim Yong Kim, nouveau président de la Banque Mondiale. " *Libération (Economie)*, 16 avril 2012. 10 Jan. 2014.
<http://www.liberation.fr/economie/2012/04/16/jim-yong-kim-nouveau-president-de-la-banque-mondiale_812101>.

L'Express, "Kofi Annan répond aux critiques dont l'ONU fait l'objet. "*l'Express, RFI, TV5*, 10 Jan. 2014.
<http://www.lexpress.fr/info/monde/dossier/onu/dossier.asp?ida=43492

Index

Kofi Annan · **14, 23, 41, 43, 49**

L

League of Nations · **11, 32**

M

Manmohan Singh · **64**
Millennium Declaration · **18**
Millennium Development Goals
(MDGs) · **23, 46**

N

National Security Agency (NSA) ·
58
Nationalism · **1, 3, 9, 86**
New Partnership for Africa's
Development, (NEPAD) · **77**
Nicolas Sarkozy · **64**

O

OAU · **18, 47, 50, 72, 76**
Osagyefo Kwame Nkrumah · **9**

R

Radio France Internationale · **14**
Regional Bureau for Education in
Africa · **24**
Reparation · **4**
Robert Mugabe · **62**
Russian Federation · **66**

S

SAP · **77**
Security Council · **19, 20, 21, 22,
28, 29, 30, 31, 32, 33, 34,
35,.36, 37, 40, 41, 42, 43, 44,
45, 46, 48, 50, 51, 54, 55, 56,
58, 59, 60, 61, 62, 64, 65, 66,
67, 68, 72, 73, 74**
South Africa · **79**
Soviet Union · **40, 41**
Sub-Saharan Africa · **9**

T

Trans-Atlantic slave trade · **9**
Trans-Saharan slave trade · **9**
TV5 · **14, 94**
TwinTowers · **52**

U

UNESCO · **24**
UNICEF · **24**
United Nations (UN) · **10, 11, 12,
13, 14, 16, 17, 18, 19, 20, 21,
22, 23, 24, 25, 26, 28, 29, 30,
31, 32, 33, 34, 35, 36, 37, 40,
41, 42, 43, 44, 45, 46, 47, 49,
50, 51, 52, 54, 55, 56, 57, 59,
60, 62, 63, 64, 66, 68, 69, 72,
74, 75**

· **4**
UN High Commissioner for
Refugees (UNHCR) · **22**
United Nations Development
Programme (UNDP) · **23**
United Nations Mission for the
Referendum in Western Sahara
(MINURSO) · **21**
United Nations Mission in Liberia

W